lcnam

Understanding the Process of Economic Change

Understanding the Process of Economic Change

Douglass C. North

PRINCETON   UNIVERSITY   PRESS

PRINCETON   AND   OXFORD

Copyright © 2005 by Princeton University Press
Published by Princeton University Press, 41 William Street,
Princeton, New Jersey 08540
In the United Kingdom: Princeton University Press,
3 Market Place, Woodstock, Oxfordshire OX20 1SY
All Rights Reserved

Library of Congress Cataloging-in-Publication Data

North, Douglass Cecil.
Understanding the process of economic change / Douglass C. North.
p.   cm.   — (Princeton economic history of the Western World)
Includes bibliographical references and index.
ISBN 0-691-11805-1 (alk. paper)
1. Evolutionary economics. 2. Economics—Sociological aspects.
3. Institutional economics. I. Title. II. Series.
HB97.3.N67   2005
330.1—dc22   2004049131

British Library Cataloging-in-Publication Data is available

This book has been composed in Minion Text

Printed on acid-free paper. ∞

pup.princeton.edu

Printed in the United States of America

10   9   8   7   6   5   4   3

Contents

Preface

UNDERSTANDING the process of economic change would enable us to account for the diverse performance of economies, past and present. We would be able to account for the long history of sustained growth of the United States and western Europe, the spectacular rise and demise of the Soviet Union, for the contrasting performances of the rapid economic growth of Taiwan and South Korea and the dismal record of sub-Saharan Africa economies, and the contrasting evolution of Latin America and of North America. And beyond understanding the past, such knowledge is the key to improving the performance of economies in the present and future. A real understanding of how economies grow unlocks the door to greater human well-being and to a reduction in misery and abject poverty.

The economic paradigm—neo-classical theory—was not created to explain the process of economic change. We live in an uncertain and ever changing world that is continually evolving in new and novel ways. Standard theories are of little help in this context. Attempting to understand economic, political, and social change (and one cannot grasp change in only one without the others) requires a fundamental recasting of the way we think. Can we develop a dynamic theory of change comparable in elegance to general equilibrium theory? The answer is probably not. But if we can achieve an understanding of the underlying process of change then we can develop somewhat more limited hypotheses about change that can enormously improve the usefulness of social science theory in confronting human problems.

This study is an extension—a very substantial extension—of the new institutional economics. A brief review of my earlier work on institutional change will provide the proper setting for that extension. From my initial studies with Lance Davis (Davis and North, 1971) and Robert Thomas (North and Thomas, 1973), I have placed institutions at the center of understanding economies because they are the incentive structure of economies. I also have focused on how economies that were composed of institutions that provided incentives for stagnation and decline could persist. The underlying source of this persistence had to be features of the human environment and of the ways humans interpreted that environment. What I did not consider in earlier studies was the character of societal change and the way humans understand and act upon that understanding of societal change.

Economic change is a process, and in this book I shall describe the nature of that process. In contrast to Darwinian evolutionary theory, the key to human evolutionary change is the intentionality of the players. The selection mechanisms in Darwinian evolutionary theory are not informed by beliefs about the eventual consequences. In contrast, human evolution is guided by the perceptions of the players; choices—decisions—are made in the light of those perceptions with the intent of producing outcomes downstream that will reduce uncertainty of the organizations—political, economic, and social—in pursuit of their goals. Economic change, therefore, is for the most part a deliberate process shaped by the perceptions of the actors about the consequences of their actions. The perceptions come from the beliefs of the players—the theories they have about the consequences of their actions—beliefs that are typically blended with their preferences.

But just how do humans come to understand their environment? The explanations that they develop are mental constructs derived from experiences, contemporary and historical. Human learning is more than the accumulation of the experiences of an individual over a lifetime. It is also the cumulative experiences of past generations. The cumulative learning of a society embodied in language, human memory, and symbol storage systems includes beliefs, myths, ways of doing things that make up the culture of a society. Culture not only determines societal performance at a moment of time but, through the way in which its scaffolding constrains the players, contributes to the process of change through time. The focus of our attention, therefore, must be on human learning—on what is learned and how it is shared among the members of a society and on the incremental process by which the beliefs and preferences change, and on the way in which they shape the performance of economies through time.

Part of the scaffolding humans erect is an evolutionary consequence of successful mutations and is therefore a part of the genetic architecture of humans, such as innate cooperation within small interacting groups; part is a consequence of cultural evolution such as the development of institutions to favor larger group cooperation. Just what is the mix between the genetic architecture and the cultural heritage is in dispute. Evolutionary psychologists have stressed the genetic component in the scaffolding process at the expense of the role of the cultural heritage. Certain universals in human mental constructs such as supernatural explanations—religions broadly construed—suggest that these are congenial to the underlying inference structure of all humans. Equally, the immense variation in the performance characteristics of societies makes clear that the cultural component of the scaffolding that humans erect is also central to the performance of economies and polities over time.

The wide gap throughout history between intentions and outcomes reflects the persistent tension between the scaffolds that humans erect to understand the human landscape and the ever changing "reality" of that landscape. That tension and its implications for the human condition both past and present, and indeed future, is the subject of this book. Part I explores the dimensions of the challenge involved in acquiring an in-depth study of the process of economic change. Part II takes us some distance along the trail toward a deeper understanding.

We cannot usefully model economic change until we understand the process. A good model entails a prior comprehension of the complex factors making up that process and then a deliberate simplifying to the crucial elements. Understanding is a necessary prerequisite missing in the economist's rush to model economic growth and change. We are a long way from completely understanding the process. Until we do, we will have very little success in deliberately improving economic performance. What follows is an attempt to improve our understanding.

This study has been a long time in process—more than ten years—and could only have developed with the generous help of many organizations and individuals.

Both Washington University, my principal location, and the Hoover Institution at Stanford, my winter home, have provided hospitable settings for research. The Mercatus Center at George Mason University and the Stanford Institute for International Studies have hosted conferences focused on issues of this book, and I am deeply indebted to Paul

Edwards and Brian Hooks of the former organization, and to Syed Shariq who played a major role in organizing the Stanford conferences.

My colleagues at Washington University have patiently put up with my endless queries and arguments. I owe particular debts to Lee and Alexandra Benham, Pascal Boyer, Randall Calvert, John Drobak, Sukoo Kim, Jack Knight, Gary Miller, John Nye, Norman Schofield, and Itai Sened.

At Stanford Paul David, Steve Haber, Avner Greif, Walter Powell, Nate Rosenberg, and Barry Weingast have been particularly helpful in furthering my education.

Participants at the conferences (in addition to those listed above) focused on issues of the book, among them Lee Alston, Robert Cooter, Leda Cosmides, Thrainn Eggertsson, Jean Ensminger, Gregory Grossman, Philip Hoffman, Timur Kuran, Chris Mantzavinos, Joel Mokyr, and Vernon Smith, were valuable to me.

I am grateful to Kevin McCabe, who in collaboration with his colleagues in the experimental laboratory at George Mason University constructed experiments to test a number of the propositions central to this study. Lengthy discussions with Andy Clark and Merlin Donald improved my understanding of many crucial issues in cognitive science.

Joel Mokyr and John Wallis read the entire manuscript and provided detailed comments; Philip Keefer did the same while working in Nepal. Peter Dougherty of the Princeton University Press also provided detailed comments on the entire manuscript. Their comments substantially improved the final draft.

My incompetence in using a computer was more than compensated for by able experts who repeatedly had to set me right—Bob Parks and Florin Petrescu in St. Louis and Dan Wilhelmi at Hoover. I am indebted to two valuable research assistants, Art Carden and Uri Sukhodolsky, and to my able secretary, Fannie Batt

My greatest debt is to Elisabeth Case, my wife, who not only edited the entire manuscript but also bore the brunt of the lengthy and sometimes traumatic gestation period of this book.

I wish to acknowledge permission to make use of the following:

By Stanford University Press, Douglass C. North, "The Paradox of the West," from R. W. Davis, ed., *Origins of Modern Freedom in the*

West, copyright 1995 by the Board of Trustees of the Leland Stanford
Jr. University.

By Yale University Press, Douglass C. North, William Summerhill,
and Barry Weingast, "Order, Disorder, and Economic Change," from
B. Bueno de Mesquita and H. Root, eds., *Governing for Prosperity,* copyright 2000 by Yale University.

An Outline of the Process of Economic Change

UNDERSTANDING economic change including everything from the rise of the Western world to the demise of the Soviet Union requires that we cast a net much broader than purely economic change because it is a result of changes (1) in the quantity and quality of human beings; (2) in the stock of human knowledge particularly as applied to the human command over nature; and (3) in the institutional framework that defines the deliberate incentive structure of a society. A complete theory of economic change would therefore integrate theories of demographic, stock of knowledge, and institutional change. We are far from having good theories of any one of these three, much less of the three together, but we are making progress. The central focus of this study, and the key to improving economic performance, is the deliberate effort of human beings to control their environment. Therefore, priority is given here to institutional change, with the consequent incentive implications for demographic and stock of knowledge changes; but there is no implication that such an approach deals adequately with the latter two.

The structure we impose on our lives to reduce uncertainty is an accumulation of prescriptions and proscriptions together with the artifacts that have evolved as a part of this accumulation. The result is a complex mix of formal and informal constraints. These constraints are imbedded in language, physical artifacts, and beliefs that together define the patterns of human interaction. If our focus is narrowly on economics, then our concern is with scarcity and, hence, competition for resources. The structure of constraints we impose to order that competition shapes the way the game is played. Because various kinds of markets (political as well as economic) have different margins at which competition can be played out, the consequence of the structure we impose will be to determine whether the competitive structure induces increasing economic efficiency or stagnation. Thus well-developed property rights that encourage productivity will increase market efficiency. The evolving structure of political and economic markets is the key to explaining performance.

While the uncertainty that pervades our existence may be reduced by the structure we impose, it is not eliminated. The constraints that we impose have, themselves, uncertain outcomes reflecting both our imperfect understanding of our environment and the equally imperfect nature of both the formal rules and the informal mechanisms we use to enforce those constraints.

This book is a study about the ceaseless efforts of humans to gain greater control over their lives and in the course of that effort continually confronting new and novel problems to solve. It is a study of the perceptions that induce institutional innovation intended to reduce uncertainty or convert uncertainty into risk. It is also a study of a continually changing human landscape. This landscape poses new challenges, as a consequence of which policies emanating from "non-rational" explanations frequently play a part in the structures we create.

I

A bare-bones description of the process of economic change is straightforward. The "reality" of a political-economic system is never known to anyone, but humans do construct elaborate beliefs about the nature of that "reality"—beliefs that are both a positive model of the way the system works and a normative model of how it should work. The belief system may be broadly held within the society, reflecting a consensus of beliefs; or widely disparate beliefs may be held, reflecting fundamental divisions in perception about the society. The dominant beliefs—those of political and economic entrepreneurs in a position to make policies—over time result in the accretion of an elaborate structure of institutions that determine economic and political performance. The resultant institutional matrix imposes severe constraints on the choice set of entrepreneurs when they seek to innovate or modify institutions in order to improve their economic or political positions. The path dependence that results typically makes change incremental although the occasional radical and abrupt institutional change suggests that something akin to the punctuated equilibrium change in evolutionary biology can occur in economic change as well. But change is continually occurring (although the rate will depend on the degree of competition among organizations and their entrepreneurs) as entrepreneurs enact policies to improve their competitive position. The result is alteration of the institutional matrix, therefore revisions of perceptions of reality, and therefore new efforts by entrepreneurs to improve their position in a never-ending process of change. The key to understanding the process of change is the intentionality of the players enacting institutional change and their comprehension of the issues. Throughout history and in the present world economic growth has been episodic because either the players' intentions have not been societal well-being or the players' comprehension of the issues has been so imperfect that the consequences have deviated radically from intention.

The nature of this overall process can be illustrated by a brief account of the rise and fall of the Soviet Union (which will be the subject of a more comprehensive analysis later). Marx and Engels provided the belief system that was Lenin's revolutionary inspiration, explaining both the way the world was and the way it should be. The circumstances of the war-torn Russia of 1917 provided the unusual opportunity for abrupt institutional change. While Marx provided no blueprint for the transformation to or construction of a socialist society, his fundamental ideological building blocks, particularly with respect to the concept of property, remained guiding principles (and constraints) of Soviet leaders. Dire necessity forced a retreat from the principles and led to the creation of the New Economic Policy (NEP) in 1921; the first five-year plan in 1928 returned to ideological orthodoxy. In the early years substantial discussion of alternative strategies and hence institutions helped shape socialism. The gradual accretion of the complex institutional matrix that resulted led to perceived successes—such as in heavy industry—and failures—such as in agriculture—and attempts to correct the failures within the belief system of Marxist orthodoxy. As the economy grew, underwent the devastating torment of the Nazi invasion, and then underwent the lengthy reconstruction process, the institutional matrix was continually being modified by external stimuli—war—or internal perceptions of needed institutional alterations guided by a belief system that evolved within the ideological limits of Marxism. The result throughout the 1950s, 1960s, and early 1970s was rapid

3

growth of physical output, military technology, and scientific knowledge; and the advent of superpower status.

Almost half the world became socialist or communist in this era and these ideologies were widely perceived to be the wave of the future. But then growth began to slow, the problems of agriculture became ever more acute, and efforts at institutional reform to rectify the problems were ineffectual. Following the advent of Gorbachev in 1985, the policies of the next six years led to absolute decline and in 1991 to the demise of the Soviet Union—perhaps the most striking case of internally induced rapid demise in all of human history.

This story of the Soviet Union is a story of perceived reality → beliefs → institutions → policies → altered perceived reality and on and on. The keys to the story are the way beliefs are altered by feedback from changed perceived reality as a consequence of the policies enacted, the adaptive efficiency of the institutional matrix—how responsive it is to alteration when outcomes deviate from intentions—and the limitations of changes in the formal rules as correctives to perceived failures.

It is one thing to be able to provide a summary description of the process of economic change; it is something else to provide sufficient content to this description to give us an understanding of this process. How well do we understand reality? How do beliefs get formed? Whose beliefs matter and how do individual beliefs aggregate into belief systems? How do they change? What is the relationship between beliefs and institutions? How do institutions change? How do institutions affect performance? What accounts for the widely varied patterns of performance of economies and polities? And perhaps most fundamental of all, what is the essential nature of the process itself? These are just a few of the questions that are the subject of this book. The remainder of this chapter elaborates on the separate parts of the puzzle.

II

What is the deep underlying force driving the human endeavor—the source of the human intentionality that comes from consciousness? It is the ubiquitous effort of humans to render their environment intelligible—to reduce the uncertainties of that environment. But the very efforts of humans to render their environment intelligible result in continual alterations in that environment and therefore new challenges to understanding that environment. The study of the process of economic change must begin therefore by exploring the ubiquitous efforts of human beings to deal with and confront uncertainty in a non-ergodic world.

Just what is it that we are trying to model in our theories, beliefs, ideologies? The pragmatic concern is with the degree to which our beliefs accord with "reality." To the extent that they do, there is some prospect that the policies that we enact will produce the intended result. But because throughout human history we have gotten it wrong (misunderstood reality) much more often than we have gotten it right (understood reality) it is important that we be very conscious about the nature of reality. Of even more importance is awareness of just how reality is changing. Beliefs and the way they evolve are at the heart of the theoretical issues of this book. For the most part, economists, with a few important exceptions such as Friedrich Hayek, have ignored the role of ideas in making choices. The rationality assumption has served economists (and other social scientists) well for a limited range of issues in micro theory but is a shortcoming in dealing with the issues central to this study.[1] Indeed the uncritical acceptance of the rationality assumption is devastating for most of the major issues confronting social scientists and is a major stumbling block in the path of future progress. The rationality assumption is not wrong, but such an acceptance forecloses a deeper understanding of the decision-making process in confronting the uncertainties of the complex world we have created.

The way we perceive the world and construct our explanations about that world requires that we delve into how the mind and brain work—the subject matter of cognitive science. This field is still in its infancy but already enough progress has been made to suggest important implications for exploring social phenomena. Issues include how humans respond to uncertainty and particularly the uncertainty arising from the changing human landscape, the nature of human learning, the relationship between human learning and belief systems, and the implica-

---

[1] See Denzau and North (1994) for a discussion of the conditions under which the rationality assumption is useful and those under which it is not.

tions of consciousness and human intentionality for the structure that humans impose on their environment.

Humans attempt to use their perceptions about the world to structure their environment in order to reduce uncertainty in human interaction. But whose perceptions matter and how they get translated into transforming the human environment are consequences of the institutional structure, which is a combination of formal rules, informal constraints, and their enforcement characteristics. This structure of human interaction determines who are the entrepreneurs whose choices matter and how such choices get implemented by the decision rules of that structure. Institutional constraints cumulate through time, and the culture of a society is the cumulative structure of rules and norms (and beliefs) that we inherit from the past that shape our present and influence our future. Institutions change, usually incrementally, as political and economic entrepreneurs perceive new opportunities or react to new threats affecting their well-being. Institutional change can result from change in the formal rules, the informal norms, or the enforcement of either of these. The political-economic structure of the society and the way it evolves is the key to whose choices matter and how they conspire to shape policies.

We can begin to put the pieces together to explore (very incompletely) the process of economic change. Is the process similar to models derived from evolutionary biology? What difference does the intentionality of the players make and what is the nature of the human intentionality that is the immediate source of institutional change? Does the uncertainty that humans face come from the inherent instability of the human landscape or from the perceptions and belief systems that we have about the human environment? What are the underlying sources of path dependence and just how does path dependence affect performance? And finally what makes for adaptive efficiency—the ability of some societies to flexibly adjust in the face of shocks and evolve institutions that effectively deal with an altered "reality"?

In part II of this book I apply the analytical framework developed in part I to attempt to provide a deeper understanding of the process of change, both historical and contemporary. I broadly outline the changes in the human landscape over the millennia since humans evolved from other primates, and particularly focus on the past two millennia. The emphasis here is on the sharp divide between institutions constructed to deal with the uncertainties that are a consequence of the physical environment and those constructed to deal with the human environment. The difficulties involved in altering the institutional framework from one geared to confronting the physical environment to one capable of dealing with the modern human environment is at the heart of many of the fundamental issues of economic development.

In the Western world, and in particular in the United States, we tend to take order for granted. We should not. Disorder—revolution, lack of personal security, chaos—has characterized a great deal of the human condition, as witness the turbulent history of Latin America. Order implies a reduction of the uncertainties that inevitably characterize the human condition as a result of institutions that provide greater predictability in human interaction. Disorder increases uncertainty as rights and privileges of individuals and organizations are "up for grabs" as a consequence of unstable relationships in both political and economic markets. Understanding the underlying conditions of order and disorder is essential for coming to grips with the process of economic change.

How successful are we at controlling our destiny? In the tradition of Herbert Simon, who directed our attention to these issues, what difference does it make that humans fall far short of substantively rational behavior, which would entail full knowledge of all possible contingencies, exhaustive exploration of the decision tree, and a correct mapping between actions, events, and outcomes? The short answer is that it makes a lot of difference. Economic history is a depressing tale of miscalculation leading to famine, starvation, defeat in warfare, death, economic stagnation and decline, and indeed the disappearance of entire civilizations. And even the most casual inspection of today's news suggests that this tale is not purely a historical phenomenon. Yet we do get it right sometimes, as the spectacular economic growth of the past few centuries attests. But ongoing success is hardly a foregone conclusion.

The beliefs and consequent institutions that produced the rise of the Western world illustrate the blend of shrewd judgments and good fortune that have gone into getting it (more or less) right. A more important objective is to tell a dynamic story—exploring the process of successful change through time. The rise and fall of the Soviet Union is a sobering exploration of the human endeavor to deliberately craft society and I explore the subject in more depth in order to elaborate two aspects of economic change: (1) the inherent difficulties involved in deliberately attempting to alter the societal framework with the very imperfect knowledge of the players, and (2) the process of disintegration of a society wrestling to overcome the rigidities and erroneous beliefs that confront societies attempting to make fundamental changes.

The accretion of experience derived from efforts to improve performance of third world and transition economies as well as what we have learned from the success stories has provided us with a crude laboratory and sobering understanding of how little we know about the process. But we are learning; and I shall describe what we have learned and what we have yet to learn in order to improve our understanding of the process.

A clear implication of understanding the nature of the process of change is the limitation the process imposes on human foresight. In this book I shall explore just how much we can know about the future and how much must remain the province of astrologers, soothsayers, and statesmen. The argument of this study suggests a sobering appraisal of the future of humans in the face of the ubiquitous uncertainty of a non-ergodic world.

PART I

THE ISSUES INVOLVED IN UNDERSTANDING

ECONOMIC CHANGE

Introduction

WHAT KIND of a theoretical framework must we develop to understand the process of economic change? The theory we possess is static; and while a truly dynamic theory may be beyond our reach we can incorporate the dimension of time as an integral part of the analysis. We must develop a body of generalizations about the operation of economies over time. Our objective must be to focus on those elements in the society that undergird and account for that process. Economics is a theory of choice—so far so good. But the discipline neglects to explore the context within which choice occurs. We choose among alternatives that are themselves constructions of the human mind. Therefore how the mind works and understands the environment is the foundation of this study. But what is the environment? The human environment is a human construct of rules, norms, conventions, and ways of doing things that define the framework of human interaction. This human environment is divided by social scientists into discrete disciplines—economics, political science, sociology—but the constructions of the human mind that we require to make sense out of the human environment do not coincide with these artificial categories. Our analytical frameworks must integrate insights derived from these artificially separate disciplines if we are to understand the process of change. Moreover we must understand what is the underlying force driving the constructs that the mind makes. Why do rules, norms, conventions, and ways of doing things exist? What induces the mind to structure human interaction in this way? The new institutional economics (NIE) takes us partway. It focuses on the beliefs that humans develop to explain their environment and the institutions (political, economic, and social) that they create to shape that environment. Part I of this book explores what drives humans to undertake these artificial constructs and then develops and expands on the tools of the NIE to provide a framework for explicitly exploring the nature of economic change.

Uncertainty in a Non-ergodic World

THE INTELLECTUAL JOURNEY on which we are embarking requires us to rethink some of the foundations of traditional economic theory, specifically those foundations dealing with the two issues that are the subject of this chapter—uncertainty and ergodicity. Economists, typically, do not ask themselves about the structure that humans impose on themselves to order their environment, and therefore reduce uncertainty; nor are they typically concerned with the dynamic nature of the world in which we live, which continues to produce novel problems to be solved. The last point raises a fundamental issue. If we are continually creating a new and novel world, how good is the theory we have developed from past experience to deal with this novel world? These questions are central to this study. We must delve into the remote sources of the forces that induce humans to devise the kind of structures that they do. It is not sufficient to describe societal change; rather we must attempt to find the underlying forces shaping the process of change.

I

Uncertainty has a long history in economic literature. It is usually traced back to Frank Knight's distinction between risk and uncertainty in a classic study published in 1921. For Knight, risk was a condition in which it was possible to derive a probability distribution of outcomes so that one could insure against such a condition. Uncertainty according to Knight was a condition in which no such probability distribution existed. Theorizing under the condition of uncertainty therefore was not possible, according to eminent theorists such as Kenneth Arrow (1951) and Robert Lucas (1981). More recently the terms have undergone some semantic alteration with uncertainty coming to mean what Knight meant by risk and the term ambiguity coming to refer to what

Knight meant by uncertainty.[1] I shall continue to use the terms as Knight defined them, although with some modification as discussed in the following paragraphs.

Economists have themselves displayed a good deal of ambiguity on the subject, largely proceeding as though uncertainty was an unusual condition and therefore the usual condition, certainty, could warrant the elegant mathematical modeling that characterizes formal economics. But uncertainty is not an unusual condition; it has been the underlying condition responsible for the evolving structure of human organization throughout history and pre-history. In order to deal properly with the issue we must define the term somewhat differently than Knight did. Knight limited his definition to a probabilistic criterion; a more general view is that humans have a ubiquitous drive to make their environment more predictable. The drive can encompass anything from rendering outcomes to be statistically probable to attempting to reduce uncertainty so fundamental in character that we do not have a clue to the possible outcomes—such as the consequences of nuclear energy for the future of humans. Ronald Heiner, in an article of fundamental importance to economic analysis, caught the essence of the issue in his assertion that uncertainty was "The Origin of Predictable Behavior" (Heiner 1983). Heiner's article points to the source of institutional innovation in what he calls the C-D gap, a gap between the agent's competence and the difficulty of the decision problem. The human agent in the face of such a gap will construct rules to restrict the flexibility of choices in such situations. We know these rules as institutions. By channeling choices into a smaller set of actions, institutions can improve the ability of the agent to control the environment (although there is no implication that the agent's perceptions are correct). Heiner directs us toward the analytical framework developed in the rest of this study. The construction of an institutional framework has been an essential building block of civilization.

The beliefs and institutions that humans have devised only make sense as an ongoing response to the various levels of uncertainty that

---

[1] There is immense literature on this subject. Good summaries of the issues and bibliographies are contained in Manski (1996) and Davidson (1991).

humans have confronted and continue to confront in the evolving physical and human landscape. While the deep underlying source of institutions has been and continues to be the effort by humans to structure the environment to make it more predictable, this effort can and frequently does make for increased uncertainty for some of the players. The development of well-specified property rights, for example, will make the overall environment more predictable but will increase uncertainty for those who traditionally have used the land in question without having formal title. Hence an essential question we must ask is, who makes the rules and for whom and what are their objectives.[2] There is no necessary identification between institutions and efficiency as economists use (and misuse) the term.[3] Indeed one of the major puzzles to be explained is how, and under what conditions, humans create the conditions that make for markets with low costs of transacting and increasing material well-being.

We can make a beginning at answering the question concerning rules by exploring the way humans have attempted to make the environment more predictable. Everyone begins life facing ubiquitous uncertainty. That initial uncertainty gets reduced by learning experiences of two kinds—those from the physical environment and those from the sociocultural linguistic environment. Experiences differ across cultures both at a moment of time and over time; humans will have different interpretations of the environment and therefore uncertainty. Therefore, knowing how learning takes place in the mind is essential for understanding how humans deal with uncertainty.

Throughout human history there has always been a large residual that defied rational explanation—a residual to be explained partly by

---

[2] It is also essential to distinguish uncertainty for an individual from uncertainty for groups in a society. While individuals are the decision makers, it is alteration of uncertainty for groups in society which is the focus of this study. However, such a distinction blurs the complex interplay between individual risk and uncertainty and community risk and uncertainty which will be explored in subsequent chapters.

[3] As I use the term efficiency throughout this work I mean a condition in which, given the state of technology and information costs, the market has the lowest production and transaction costs attainable. The term is almost always used in relative rather than absolute terms. Moreover, while in economic markets efficiency would coincide

non-rational explanations embodied in witchcraft, magic, religions; but partly by more prosaic non-rational behavior characterized by dogmas, prejudices, "half-baked" theories.[4] Indeed despite the above cited assertion by eminent theorists that it is not possible to theorize in the face of uncertainty, humans do it all the time; their efforts range from ad-hoc assertions and loosely structured beliefs such as those encompassed in the labels "conservative" and "liberal" to elegant systematic ideologies such as Marxism or organized religions.

A general characteristic of human history has been the systematic reduction in the perceived uncertainty associated with the physical environment and therefore a reduction in those sources of uncertainty to be explained by beliefs embodied in witchcraft, magic, and religions. But if uncertainty associated with the physical environment has declined, a consequence has been a vastly more complex human environment. And while we have made some progress in understanding this human environment, our understanding is very limited and characterized by an immense amount of non-rational explanation. Part of the reason for our limited understanding is that there do not appear to be any fundamental "power laws" in the social sciences comparable to those in the physical sciences. A more fundamental reason is the non-ergodic nature of the world we are continually altering. An ergodic economy is one in which the fundamental underlying structure of the economy is constant and therefore timeless. But the world we live in is non-ergodic—a world of continuous novel change; and comprehending the world that is evolving entails new theory, or at least modification of that which we possess. In consequence, there is no implication that we "have it right" despite the awesome advances in science which have enormously reduced uncertainty about the physical environment. With this caveat in mind, let us see how humans through time have altered the environment to make it more predictable. We go back to the definition of uncertainty and divide the term into different degrees:

---

with improved material well-being, in political markets the welfare implications are more ambiguous, as I shall demonstrate in chapter 5.

[4] By rational I mean explanations that are logically consistent and in principle subject to empirical verification.

1. Uncertainty that can be reduced by increasing information given the existing stock of knowledge.[5]

2. Uncertainty that can be reduced by increasing the stock of knowledge within the existing institutional framework.

3. Uncertainty that can be reduced only by altering the institutional framework.

4. Uncertainty in the face of novel situations that entails restructuring beliefs.

5. Residual uncertainty that provides the foundation for "non-rational" beliefs.

A major challenge to economic historians would be to write economic history exploring each of these historical processes. Here is a brief elaboration of each of these categories:

1. The development of more information about the characteristics of a human activity has led to predictability. For example, in the fifteenth century the development of marine insurance which entailed collecting and collating information on ships, cargoes, destinations, time en route, wrecks, damage, converted uncertainty into risk. It was a major factor in increasing trade in early modern Europe.

2. Increase in the stock of knowledge has been the fundamental source of increased human well-being.[6] Some of this increase has occurred without a change in the institutional structure being the source of the altered incentives. Increasing the stock of knowledge within the existing institutional framework has occurred throughout history as a consequence of the ubiquitous drive of humans to invent and innovate even in the absence of institutional incentives, as an impressive account of human creativity throughout the ages attests. Other major sources of increases in the stock of knowledge have been changing relative prices or alterations in beliefs, both leading to resource reallocations. Fundamental changes in the relative prices of factors of production have, throughout history, altered incentives to acquire knowledge about those

---

[5] I define knowledge as the accumulation of regularities and patterns in the physical and human environment that result in organized explanations of aspects of those environments. There is no implication that such knowledge is "true."

[6] For a thoughtful discussion of knowledge, useful knowledge, and its relationship to economic performance see Mokyr (2002).

productive factors. For example, the Neolithic revolution and the onset of the plague in fourteenth-century Europe led to both fundamental societal reorganization and redirection of resources and the acquisition of knowledge (see North 1981, chapters 7 and 10). As for changes in beliefs, it is finally ideas and their creation which for good and sometimes for evil are the fundamental driving force of the human condition and are the major focus of this study.

3. Altering the institutional framework entails changing the incentive structure and has been an essential condition for the reduction in the uncertainties of the environment over time. It has been the major tool by which humans have attempted deliberately to alter their environment. It encompasses many of the efforts in the contemporary world to improve the performance of third world economies. Historically, institutional change has altered the pay-off to cooperative activity (the legal enforcement of contracts, for example), increased the incentive to invent and innovate (patent laws), altered the pay-off to investing in human capital (the development of institutions to integrate the distributed knowledge of complex economies), and lowered transaction costs in markets (the creation of a judicial system that lowers the costs of contract enforcement).

4. The response of humans to novel situations depends on how novel they are and on the cultural heritage of the actors. Their cultural heritage will, in many instances, determine the success or lack of success of the actors. To the extent that that cultural heritage has equipped them to deal with such problems they may, in fact, make responses that make that environment more predictable. If they have not been so equipped they may make inappropriate responses or relegate the issue to witchcraft and/or similar anti-rational responses. The differential response of economies to the move from personal to impersonal exchange is illustrative. Economies that had evolved a cultural heritage that led them to innovate institutions of impersonal exchange dealt successfully with this fundamental novelty. Those with no such heritage failed, as Avner Greif has documented (forthcoming a).

5. Despite the fact that uncertainty associated with the physical environment has been radically reduced (although resulting in increased uncertainty about the human environment) the residual that leads to non-rational beliefs plays a major role in the world today as it has all

through history. The history of and the widespread belief in religions is illustration. Religious belief systems such as Islamic fundamentalism have played and continue to play a major role in shaping societal change; but equally significant is the critical role of secular ideologies and belief systems in decision making, as the rise and decline of the Soviet Union so vividly illustrates.

II

Ergodic is defined in Webster's dictionary as "involving or relating to the probability that any state will recur, especially having zero probability that any state will never recur." Therefore, "an ergodic stochastic process simply means that averages calculated from past observations cannot be persistently different from the time average of future outcomes" (Davidson 1991, 132). For Samuelson the ergodic hypothesis was essential for a scientific economics (Samuelson 1969, 184). And indeed the ergodic hypothesis is implicit in much of current economic theory. Robert Solow, in discussing the fundamental assumptions of economic theory, characterized such a view as follows: "My impression is that the best and the brightest in the profession proceed as if economics is the physics of society. There is a single universally valid model of the world. It only needs to be applied" (Solow 1985, 330).

To an economic historian surveying the ten millennia of human history from the onset of the Neolithic revolution, however, the ergodic hypothesis is a-historical. Further, the extraordinary changes in every facet of present-day society are evident all around us; and it is evident that we have been and are creating societies that are unique in comparison to anything in the past.

The physical sciences resort to reduction to arrive at the fundamental underlying principles that makes their science (maybe) ergodic. The social sciences have no such underlying principles except perhaps a behavioral assumption and even that turns out to be far from satisfactory, as research in cognitive science demonstrates. But the reverse position is equally untenable—that the theory derived from past experience has no relevance for understanding the present and the future. Microeconomic theory has repeatedly demonstrated its power to explain (and predict) aspects of economic performance. What we must sort out are the kinds of theory and their appropriateness in particular contexts in a non-ergodic world. But first let us be sure that we understand the essential characteristics of a non-ergodic world.

Exactly what is it that is changing all the time? Is it the physical world? Yes, that is changing, but our subject matter is the human environment. And we have made immense strides at rendering that environment more predictable today. Can we, therefore, predict what it will be like tomorrow? The answer is that the time horizon for such prediction to be accurate is very short. The changes in the environment that we make today create a new and in many cases novel environment tomorrow—novel in the sense that we have no historical experience that prepares us to deal with it. We return to the elaborations in the previous section:

1. The advent of marine insurance was a major step in expanding international trade and the integration of the world economies but with downstream implications that surely would have inspired awe in a fifteenth-century merchant.

2. The consequences of the evolving technology of warfare have, throughout history, produced societal changes that were not and could not have been predicted. At a more micro level, there is Schumpeter's insight about the creative destruction characteristics of innovation having continually produced unanticipated changes not only in the specific product being revolutionized but in its larger ramifications for societal change—the consequences of the automobile in the past century, for example. The Neolithic revolution and the fourteenth-century plague both set in motion fundamental alterations in societies of monumental proportions. And as for changing beliefs, they are the fundamental force for change—some anticipated but most not anticipated.

3. The alteration of institutions that has led to the reduction in the uncertainties of the physical environment has created the complex human environment which has produced a whole new (and in many cases still unresolved) set of uncertainties. The revolution in technology of the past several centuries has made possible a level of human well-being of unimaginable proportions as compared to the past, but it also has produced a world of interdependence and universal externalities, and in consequence a whole new set of uncertainties. The law merchant,

patent laws, the institutional integration of distributed knowledge, the creation of a judicial system, have been important parts of efforts making markets more efficient in developed countries. And they are leading us into an unknown world of future uncertainties. When such institutional changes are applied to third world economies they frequently alter income distribution and produce political instability, sometimes leading to downstream consequences that are the very reverse of the intended objective.

4. and 5. But how do humans deal with true novelty? If the nature of the non-ergodic condition is such that the historical experience of the players has equipped them to deal with the problem (uncertainty of the first three kinds) they may deal with it effectively. In the case of true novelty, however, we have uncertainty and we simply do not know what the outcomes may be; then the likelihood of successful reduction of uncertainty is just luck and the players will resort to non-rational beliefs. And indeed non-rational beliefs play a big part in societal change.

What the foregoing point suggests is that path dependence—the way by which institutions and beliefs derived in the past influence present choices—plays a crucial role in this flexibility. Societies whose past experiences conditioned them to regard innovative change with suspicion and antipathy are in sharp contrast to those whose heritage provided a favorable milieu to such change. Underlying such diverse cultural heritages are the shared mental models of the participants in each case.

The future will reflect our understanding (both the rational and non-rational) of ourselves, which continues to undergo change as we alter our human (and physical) environment. To know the future we would have to know today what we will know tomorrow. To achieve a better understanding of where we are going we must necessarily focus on the way in which the mind works and makes sense of our external environment. The ideas and, more structured, the beliefs we humans hold shape the decisions we make that keep altering that environment. When we combine the issues arising from imperfect perception with issues arising from non-ergodicity we arrive at the following combinations that are at the heart of this study:[7]

---

[7] I am indebted to my colleague Sukoo Kim for elaborating on these distinctions.

1. Perfect perception:

   a. Static uncertainty—At any time there are states of the world in which no probability distribution can be defined. In a static world uncertainty is a function of the stock of knowledge. If individuals have perfect perception, then there may not be any need for institutions even in the face of uncertainty. If this static world is repeated over time then it may be plausible that states of uncertainty would go to zero.

   b. Uncertainty in an ergodic world—The only difference between this and static uncertainty might be that the states of uncertainty are randomly generated. Thus over time there may always be some residual level of uncertainty.

   c. Uncertainty in a non-ergodic world—Systematic relationships may change over time in unpredictable ways. Thus, new, fundamentally different uncertainties may arise. Even if agents had perfect perception at any time, given the history of the world, their action might turn out to be flawed at another. Thus new levels of uncertainty always arise. In some sense knowledge depreciates in value over time.

2. Imperfect perception:

   a-b. Static uncertainty and uncertainty in an ergodic world—If agents' perception of the environment is imperfect, then it may be possible that uncertainty may persist even if the static uncertainty case is replicated over time. This result depends a great deal on whether agents have an optimal learning rule. An agent's imperfect perception can be defined as having a wrong probability distribution of risk-states or assigning probability over uncertainty-states. Non-rational beliefs are likely to be of the latter sort; that is, they assign certain probability on states of uncertainty for which no such probability can be "reasonably" assigned. In a world of imperfect perception, uncertainty is a function of knowledge and institutions.

   c. Uncertainty in a non-ergodic world—The major change here is that institutions adopted for a particular time, even if optimal (that is, correct perception) at that time, may be far from optimal as the human environment changes over time. How humans deal with such novel developments is a major part of this study.

CHAPTER THREE

Belief Systems, Culture, and Cognitive Science

As soon as we realize that we always have an imperfect grasp of "reality" and frequently have contrasting and conflicting views of the human landscape, we can begin to get a handle on the process of human change. The process works as follows: the beliefs that humans hold determine the choices they make that, in turn, structure the changes in the human landscape. How humans perceive the human landscape, how they learn, and what they learn is the subject of this chapter. We begin with exploring the mind of the individual as a necessary condition to understanding societal beliefs.

The rationality assumption underlies economic (and increasingly other social science) theory. There is an immense literature on both the usefulness and the limitations of this behavioral assumption.[1] The substantive rationality assumption of the economist works well in competitive posted-price markets. The competitive environment so structures the situation that price can effectively be viewed as a parameter and only the quantity to buy or sell need be chosen. If all choices were simple, were made frequently, had substantial and rapid feedback, and involved substantial motivation, then substantive rationality would suffice for all purposes. The rationality assumption would be both a predictive and a descriptive model of equilibrium settings, and learning models based upon it could be used to describe the dynamics out of equilibrium. But as soon as we move away from this simple competitive model and the price depends on the behavior of other buyers and sellers the complexity of the decision increases and we need to delve much more deeply into the cognitive process. In particular we must take account of the ubiquitous existence of uncertainty as discussed in the previous chapter. The tendency of economists to carry over the rationality assumption in undi-

---

[1] See Hogarth and Reder (1987) for the proceedings of an interdisciplinary conference held on the subject.

23

luted form to more complex issues involving uncertainty has been a roadblock to improving our understanding of the human landscape.

The interesting issues that require resolution come from the interaction of human beings in economic, social, and political settings in which the players are imperfectly informed and the feedback on their actions is likewise imperfect. It is not that the rationality assumption is "wrong." Rather it is that it does not provide us with a guide to understanding the choices humans make in a variety of crucial contexts that are fundamental to the process of change. Imperfect information and feedback underlie the ubiquitous character of uncertainty; in addition, the rationality assumption fails to deal adequately with the relationship of the mind to the environment. The former point is the subject of chapter 2, but the latter requires amplification.

I

"Every thought is had by a brain. But the flow of thoughts and the adaptive success of reason are now seen to depend on repeated and crucial interactions with external sources. The role of such interactions . . . is clearly computational and informational: it is to transform inputs, to simplify search, to aid recognition, to prompt associative recall, to offload memory, and so on. . . . Brain and world collaborate in ways richer and more clearly driven by computational and informational needs than was previously suspected" (Clark 1997, 68–69). The implication of this assertion for social science theorizing is that much of what passes for rational choice is not so much individual cogitation as the embeddedness of the thought process in the larger social and institutional context. Satz and Ferejohn (1994, 72) conclude that "the [traditional] theory of rational choice is most powerful in contexts where choice is limited." Clark (1997, 182) explains: "When the external scaffolding of policies, infrastructure and customs is strong and (importantly) is a result of competitive selection, the individual members are, in effect, interchangeable cogs in a larger machine. The larger machine extends way outside the individual, incorporating large-scale social, physical, and even geopolitical structures. And it is the diffused reasoning and behavior of this larger machine that traditional economic theory often succeeds in modeling." We seek a better, if imperfect, grasp of the complex interaction between cognitive processes, belief formation, and institutions.

II

It would be nice to be able to say that cognitive science has developed far enough to give us an unambiguous guide to the issues posed at the beginning of this chapter. It has not; but it has come a long way in a short period of time and provides the promise of dealing ever more authoritatively with the issues in the future.[2]

Broadly, the process of human learning can be described as a cognitive process, as follows:

> Learning entails developing a structure by which to interpret the various signals received by the senses. The initial architecture of the structure is genetic, but the subsequent scaffolding is a result of the experiences of the individual—experiences coming from the physical environment and from the socio-cultural linguistic environment. The structure consists of categories—classifications that gradually evolve from earliest childhood to organize our perceptions and keep track of our memory of analytic results and experiences. Building on these classifications, we form mental models to explain and interpret the environment—typically in ways relevant to some goal. Both the categories and mental models will evolve reflecting the feedback derived from new experiences: feedback that sometimes strengthens our initial categories and models or may lead to modifications—in short learning. Thus the mental models may be continually redefined with new experiences, including contacts with others' ideas.[3]

According to a perceptive essay on "Learning in Evolutionary Environments" (Dosi et al. forthcoming), an evolutionary theory of learning would have the following building blocks:

[2] See Baumgartner and Sabine (1996) for an excellent summary of the state of the field which highlights disagreements as well as accomplishments.

[3] North (1994, 362–63). Still the best overall approach to the field is Holland et al. (1986).

25

cognitive foundations focused on the dynamics of categories and mental
    models;

heuristics as quite general processes for decision and learning;

context-dependence, and, relatedly, social embeddedness of both inter-
    pretative models and decision rules;

endogeneity of (possibly inconsistent) goals and preferences;

organizations as behavioral entities in their own right;

processes of learning, adaptation and discovery apt to (imperfectly) guide
    representations and behaviors also (or primarily?) in ever changing
    environments.

Issues about the cognitive process are far from resolved. Does the
brain operate like a computer or does it operate by a process of somatic
selection?[4] I am not qualified to judge among the alternatives currently
being advanced by neuroscientists. In this chapter I explore a connectionist model in order to lay out the issues which are at stake.[5] It is
important for subsequent argument in this book that both connectionist models and selection models view the brain as employing pattern-based reasoning, which is essential for explaining choices in a
world of uncertainty. Pattern recognition rather than abstract logical
reasoning is at base the way human neural networks appear to operate.
"Thinking occurs in terms of synthesized patterns, not logic, and for
this reason it may always exceed in its reach syntactical or mechanical
relations" (Edelman and Tonini 2001, 152). Such an approach is consistent with research on the nature of human learning. Much of learning
comes from absorbing and adjusting to subtle events that have an impact on our lives, incrementally modifying our behavior ever so slightly.
Implicit knowledge evolves without ever being reasoned out. In fact we

[4] See Edelman and Tononi (2001, 212–18) for an excellent summary of the issues.

[5] Connectionist models are neural network models of perceptual or cognitive processes which obtain and manufacture their representations of reality. "Artificial neural
nets acquire experience by changing their connectionist patterns after repeated exposures to the environment. They form impressions in essentially the same way a time-
exposed astronomical photograph does, by passively gathering data over time. Several
exposures to an object allow neural networks to extract consistencies in the world that
relate to the object. These are stored in stable connection patterns" (Donald 2001, 155).
For a criticism of the foundations of connectionist theory see Edelman (1992, 226–27).

are relatively poor at reasoning compared to our ability to understand problems and see solutions. We are good at understanding and comprehending if the issue is sufficiently similar to other events that have happened in our experience. Ideas too far from the norms embodied in our culture cannot easily be incorporated into our culture. Ideas are adopted if and when they share a kind of cohesion that does not take them too far from the norms we possess. Pattern matching is the way we perceive, remember, and comprehend. This is the key to our ability to generalize and use analogy. This ability makes us good not only at modeling "reality," but also at constructing theories in the face of real uncertainty.

An experiment undertaken by the psychologist Julian Feldman draws out some of the implications of pattern recognition for theorizing in the face of uncertainty. "Feldman had subjects predict which of two events, the appearance of a '1' symbol or the appearance of a '0' symbol would occur next in a sequence of two hundred trials where the experimenter could control whether 1 or 0 appeared next. . . . Feldman found that each subject was quick to spot patterns in the sequence of 1's and 0's and to form hypotheses on the process generating the sequence. . . . The interesting point is that the sequence of 1's and 0's used was perfectly random. Yet each subject could 'see' patterns to act upon, albeit different ones as the experiment progressed."[6] Finding patterns where none exist is consistent with the ubiquitous effort of human beings to have explanations, theories, dogmas to explain the world around them even in the absence of a "scientific" explanation. Indeed it may be a superior survival trait to have any explanation rather than no explanation for the problems we confront.

The process of learning is unique to each individual but a common institutional/educational structure (the subject of chapter 5) will result in shared beliefs and perceptions. A common cultural heritage, therefore, provides a means of reducing the divergent mental models that people in a society possess and constitutes the means for the intergenerational transfer of unifying perceptions.[7]

---

[6] Reported by Brian Arthur (1992).

[7] For a further discussion of the unifying role of a common cultural heritage see Denzau and North (1994).

Before going further we should consider two still unresolved controversies that bear on the issues in this study. They concern the degree to which the genetic architecture of the mind shapes special features of human cognition and the fundamental characteristics of the cognitive process.

III

The first controversy squarely addresses the issue of to what degree the genetic architecture of the mind, in contrast to environmental conditioning, shapes cultures. Evolutionary psychologists have asserted that the millions of years of hunter/gatherer conditions have resulted in the genetic development of special purpose adaptations of the mind that are responsible for much of our cultural characteristics.

> The claim that our only evolved psychological mechanisms are general-purpose and content-free, and that "culture" must therefore supply all the specific content of our minds, is exactly the issue on which evolutionary psychological approaches diverge most sharply from more traditional ones. In our view instead of culture manufacturing the psychology of social exchange de novo, content-specific evolved psychologies constitute the building blocks out of which cultures themselves are manufactured. (Tooby and Cosmides 1992, 207–8)

Yet evolutionary biologists like Stephen J. Gould have maintained that there is a lot of slack in the genetic architecture, which provides much more latitude for environmental conditioning. Gould maintained not only that the selection environment changes but that in many cases it is relatively "loose," resulting in survivals in which chance and breeding capabilities rather than competitive pressures may play a major role.

At issue is the adaptability of the human mind. The evolutionary psychologist would have much of cooperative human behavior genetically determined and some recent empirical research by experimental economists lends some support to this argument. Elizabeth Hoffman, Kevin McCabe, and Vernon Smith (1998, 350) summarize a large number of experimental game results as follows:

[P]eople invoke reward/punishment strategies in a wide variety of small group interactive contexts. These strategies are generally inconsistent with, but more profitable than, the noncooperative strategies predicted by game theory. There is, however, consistency with the game theoretic folk theorem which asserts that repetition favors cooperation, although we observe a substantial use of reward/punishment strategies and some achievement of cooperative outcomes in single play games. Non cooperative outcomes are favored, however, where it is very costly to coordinate outcomes, in large groups, and even in smaller groups under private information. In large groups interacting through markets using property rights and a medium of exchange, and with disperse private information, non-cooperative interaction supports the achievement of socially desirable outcomes. Experimental studies have long supported this fundamental theorem of markets. This theorem does not generally fail, however, in small group interactions because people modify their strict self-interest behavior, using reward/punishment strategies that enable some approximation of surplus maximizing outcomes. Seen in the light of evolutionary psychology, such behavior is not a puzzle, but a natural product of our mental evolution and social adaptation.

The evolutionary psychologists' argument is not new. It is a continuation (if with some additional interesting empirical research) of the arguments of sociobiologists such as Edward Wilson who has restated his position with elegance in a recent study arguing for a unified approach to knowledge built on the physical sciences (Wilson 1998). Certainly no one would quarrel with his central thesis that "Behavior is guided by epigenetic rules" where "Epigenesis, originally a biological concept, means the development of an organism under the joint influence of heredity and environment" (Wilson 1998, 193). But for the social scientist attempting to account for the enormous diversity in the human condition both historically and in the contemporary world, such features as the universal taboo against incest, the innate language capability of humans, and even the propensity for cooperative behavior—all viewed as genetic features by Wilson, Chomsky (1975), and Pinker (1994), and by Tooby and Cosmides—while important building blocks in epigenesis, take us a short, if significant, distance in understanding the human condition and the process of change. The most important contribution of the evolutionary psychologist is explicating

29

the underlying inference structure of the mind that appears to account for the predisposition of the mind to entertain and construct "non-rational" beliefs such as supernatural explanations and religions that underlie so much of the decision framework of individuals, groups, and organizations in societies.[8] The immense variation, however, in the performance characteristics of political/economic units over time makes clear that the Lamarkian characteristics of culture must also be central to the understanding of the process. The exact mixture between the genetic predispositions and the cultural imperatives is far from resolved, however, and represents an important frontier for further research.

IV

The second controversy concerns such questions as, how does the mind work? What are the basic "operating mechanisms" of the mind and how are they accomplished by the brain? The early work in artificial intelligence (AI) built on the computer analogy; more recent work built around a parallel distributed processing model, while still influenced by the computer analogy, has gone in a different direction. In this section I follow a connectionist model in exploring the issues of how knowledge is stored and retrieved. The artificial intelligence approach operates under the assumption that knowledge is stored and retrieved in memory like data in computer storage. Connectionist theory, in contrast, would not simulate cognitive processes by means of symbols and symbolic manipulation, as in the artificial intelligence model; but rather would simulate the process taking place in neural systems in the brain. The resultant artificial neural networks are, at best, crude models of the very complex structure of the brain but suggest a very different way of storing and retrieving knowledge—although Paul Smolensky suggests that the two approaches are compatible.[9]

[8] See Boyer (2001) for an invaluable discussion.

[9] The issues are far from resolved. Excellent discussions are contained in Bechtel and Graham, eds. (1998). In particular see the essay by Robert Mccauley, "Levels of Explanation and Cognitive Architecture." Smolensky's views are discussed on page 621.

The contrast between the classic and the connectionist approach leads us to the mechanisms by which the mind and intelligence systems operate. Do the cognitive processes entail the use, manipulation, and storage of internal representations? "Since cognitive processes are assumed to be computational processes, explaining how an intelligent system works requires some computational framework. The link between computationalism and representationalism appears to be direct, for without a medium of internal representations, computational systems could not compute" (Stufflebeam 1998, 640). But in a connectionist framework the networks could learn the value of the weights to be assigned by an inductive process. This process would, by trial and error, arrive at weights which connectionist theorists have simulated by a number of learning algorithms. "In effect a neurally-inspired computer 'network' learns to recognize patterns by adjusting local thresholds of activation on a wide range of individual computational units each of them quite stupid. The idea is that although individual units are stupid, the overall network can be quite smart" (Turner 2001, 138). Merlin Donald summarizes our state of understanding of connectionist models very well as follows: "The reason connectionist models are attractive is that they try to model the brain and mind with a non-symbolic (sometimes called a non-representational) strategy. Like a primitive nervous system, a connectionist network constructs its own perceptual version of the world, without relying on a symbolic system given to it by a human operator. Such models are very rudimentary at present, but in principle they could be made much more powerful" (1991, 366).

If the latter is a correct understanding of the mechanism it has important implications for the process of learning. Connectionist models learn by example and "use the statistics of those examples to drive learning. The attraction of the approach is that although learning is statistically driven, the outcome of the learning process is a system whose knowledge is generalizable to novel instances" (Elman 1998, 496). But the generalizability of knowledge leads us to a further critical issue. It is one thing to be able to account for innate predispositions (such as Chomsky on grammar or classical AI models) as sources of learning and to further attribute learning to interaction between the physical and socio-cultural/linguistic environment, but how does the mind enrich itself from within by exploiting the knowledge that it has already represented? Clark and Karmiloff-Smith (1993) argue that the mind appears to order and reorder the mental models from their special purpose origins to successively more abstract form so that they become available to process other information. The capacity to generalize from the particular to the general and to use analogy is a part of what they term representational redescription and underlies not only creative thinking but belief systems generally. But exactly how representational redescription works is a matter of some controversy, as subsequent comments on the Clark and Karmiloff-Smith article demonstrated.[10]

If we move from the mind to the brain, a necessary step for further understanding, we encounter still less understood puzzles. While new techniques for brain imaging (neuroimaging techniques) have increased our understanding of (and added a few new puzzles to) the operation of neural networks in mental processes, there is still much that is not understood.[11] In fact, it is only quite recently that brain and mind scientists have come together to enrich their understanding. For example, neurons in the brain are separated by synapses and communication across synapses is mediated by chemicals. "These have been shown to be critical to normal cognition, but a detailed understanding of how they figure in cognition remains to be developed" (Bechtel et al. 1998, 95).

These controversies are unresolved, but we can do much with the tools and understanding that we possess.

V

The place to begin to build an integrated approach to the issues raised at the beginning of this chapter is with an acknowledgement of Friedrich Hayek, whose book *The Sensory Order* (1952) pioneered in developing

---

[10] See commentary on Karmiloff-Smith, Beyond Modularity (1994).

[11] For a thoughtful and imaginative exploration of the interplay between brain and mind and its implications for consciousness see Damasio (1999). Edelman (1992) is an impressive, and controversial, attempt to integrate an evolutionary theory of the brain (which he calls neural Darwinism) with a theory of consciousness. I shall build on their studies in the next chapter.

an understanding of the process of learning and the formation of beliefs long before cognitive scientists had developed connectionist theory. For Hayek beliefs are a construction of the mind as interpreted by the senses. We do not reproduce reality; rather we construct systems of classifications to interpret the external environment. "Perception is thus always an interpretation, the placing of something into one or several classes of objects. . . . The qualities which we attribute to the experienced objects are strictly speaking not properties of that object at all, but a set of relationships by which our nervous system classifies them or, to put it differently, all we know about the world is of the nature of theories and all experience can do is to change those theories" (Hayek 1952, 143).

For Hayek the mind is inseparably connected with the environment. "The apparatus by means of which we learn about the external world is itself the product of a kind of experience. It is shaped by the conditions prevailing in the environment in which we live, and it represents a kind of generic reproduction of the relations between the elements of this environment which we have experienced in the past; and we interpret any new event in the environment in the light of that experience" (ibid., 165). It follows that the experiences that have shaped the mental classifications in the mind can and frequently will lead to misinterpretations of the problems confronting the individual. "The classification of the stimuli performed by our senses will be based on a system of acquired connections which reproduce, in a partial and imperfect manner, relations existing between the corresponding physical stimuli. The 'model' of the physical world which is thus formed will give only a very distorted reproduction of the relationships existing in that world; and the classification of these events by our senses will often prove to be false, that is, give rise to expectations that will not be borne out by events" (ibid., 145).

Hayek's views have an amazingly modern resonance in recent work in cognitive science. Edwin Hutchins[12] argues that we cannot adequately understand cognition without accounting for the fact that "culture, context, and history . . . are fundamental aspects of human cognition and cannot be comfortably integrated into a perspective that privileges

[12] Hutchins (1995, 354). This section draws from Knight and North (1997).

abstract properties of isolated individual minds." The basic task is one of "locating cognitive activity in context, where context is not a fixed set of surrounding conditions but a wider dynamical process of which the cognition of the individual is only a part" (1995, xiii). By accomplishing this task we can "show that human cognition is not just influenced by culture and society, but that it is in a very fundamental sense a cultural and social process" (ibid., xiv).

The fundamental building blocks of a culture begin with language whose categories and vocabulary reflect the cumulative experience of a society. Merlin Donald asserts that "Other species start at basically the same level with each new generation; not so humans. Semantic content and even the cultural algorithms that support certain kinds of thinking can accumulate, and the symbolic environment can affect the way individual brains deploy their resources. The process of enculturation must have started very slowly, presumably with very gradual increments to a primate knowledge-base, but has evidently accelerated in an exponential manner in the modern period" (Donald 1991, 12). Donald proposes successive stages in the evolution of primate/hominid culture using a cognitive criterion for classification. The first stage, labeled Episodic, characterizes primates. Apes are intelligent (as an immense amount of recent empirical research attests) but have a limited range of expressive outputs. This limitation must initially have been overcome by an increase in motor skills characterizing what he labels the Mimetic stage. "A second hominid cognitive transition led from mimetic culture to speech and a fully-developed oral-mythic culture. This emerged over the past several hundred thousand years culminating in the speciation of modern Homo Sapiens. Oral culture is a specialized adaptation that complements but does not replace the functions served by mimetic culture" (ibid., 14). He labels this stage Mythic because it is characterized by a shared narrative tradition with language becoming a universal trait. It is the possession of developed language that sets humans apart and underlies the dynamics of cultural change. The final, Theoretic, stage of symbolically literate societies "has been marked by a long, and culturally cumulative, history of visuosymbolic invention" (ibid., 15). Symbolic invention did not trigger new innate mental capacities. "Rather, the new representational possibilities emerged from a developed symbiosis with the external symbolic environment, the basis for a particularly radical form of enculturation" (ibid.). It is this last development that provides the foundation for the modern dynamic interplay between the mind and its external environment. It is worth quoting Donald on the implications of a "theoretic" culture:

> Theoretic culture is the realm of the professional and the theoretician, and its institutional structure depends on high levels of symbolic literacy, which, in its broadest definition, includes all the mental skills that are relevant to the effective use of symbolic systems. Theories emerge from pursuing the algorithms stored in these disciplines. Once developed, they are usually preserved in permanent form in various external memory media, such as legal codices. Theoretic culture is a large subsection of the larger culture. It engages many thousands of individuals whose lives are lived in its service. It includes many theoretic domains, including management, political and legal systems, and other specializations. These domains share the principle that, whatever their area of expertise, theories rule. (2000, 4)

The development of the "scientific method"—the use of statistical techniques and the sophisticated interaction of theory and empirical evidence—transformed our understanding of the physical and human environment. Theoretic culture underlies Hutchins's vision of the culture of a society as encompassing a computational system of continuous interaction between mind and external structure. He illustrates this view by a lengthy account of navigating a ship into San Pedro harbor:

> The basic computations of navigation could be characterized at the computational, representational/algorithmic, and implementational levels entirely in terms of observable representations. On this view of cognitive systems, communication among the actors is seen as a process internal to the cognitive system. Computational media, such as diagrams and charts, are seen as representations internal to the system, and the computations carried out upon them are more processes internal to the system. Because the cognitive activity is distributed across a social network, many of these internal processes and internal communications are directly observable. (Hutchins 1995, 128–29)

On this view "the proper unit of analysis for talking about cognitive change includes the socio-material environment of thinking. Learning is adaptive reorganization in a complex system" (ibid., 289). For Hutchins, like Hayek, culture is an adaptive process that accumulates partial solutions to frequently encountered problems of the past. Such an approach highlights the important cognitive role of social institutions. The enhanced specification of how individual beliefs interrelate with social context provides a set of mechanisms by which culture and social institutions enter more directly into explanations of economic change. We can only make sense of the contrasting characteristics of societies like those of the Muslim world and those of the Western world in terms of an in-depth exploration of the interrelationship between the evolving belief systems and their social contexts, as we shall elaborate in part II of this book.

When we move from Hutchins's dynamic social group embodied in a navigation team to the larger implications for the structure, functioning, and process of change for a whole society we can see that the cultural heritage provides the artifactual structure—beliefs, institutions, tools, instruments, technology—which not only plays an essential role in shaping the immediate choices of players in a society but also provides us with clues to the dynamic success or failure of societies through time. In essence, the richer the artifactual structure, the greater the reduction of uncertainty in making choices at a moment of time. Over time, the richer the cultural context in terms of providing multiple experimentation and creative competition, the more likely the successful survival of the society. These generalizations require careful elaboration and qualification, but they are a foundation of this study.

The richer the artifactual structure, the wider the range of routine decisions that can be made. In effect the game has been structured to relieve the individual of uncertainty in choice making. In contrast, an environment in disorder is one in which routines have been disrupted and uncertainty increased. Modern western societies like the United States embody a rich cultural heritage which has led to the immensely complex artifactual structure that not only gives us command over nature in an unparalleled fashion but equally extends our range of "easy" decision making over space and time in ways that would be beyond the comprehension of our ancestors. In effect this artifactual structure has converted uncertainty into certainty or at least risk over an ever wider domain of human activity. The contrast between making everyday choices in a developed society like the United States and making those choices in an undeveloped society is a sobering testimonial to the significance of possessing a rich artifactual structure.

But if humans have extended their grasp over their environment they *ENTREPRENEUR S* have done so by continually reaching out into the unknown; sometimes they are successful, thereby widening the horizons of human control, and sometimes they fail and arrested development, decline, or human demise is the consequence. We seek to understand the conditions that can increase the likelihood of human success when confronting novel situations.

Antonio Damasio elegantly states the implications of the neurobiological foundations of the self that underlie cognition in the conclusion of his study *The Feeling of What Happens*:

> The drama of the human condition comes solely from consciousness. Of course consciousness and its revelations allow us to create a better life for self and others, but the price we pay for that better life is high. It is not just the price of knowing risk, danger, and pain. Worse even: it is the price of knowing what pleasure is and knowing when it is missing or unattainable.
>
> The drama of the human condition thus comes from consciousness because it concerns knowledge obtained in a bargain that none of us struck: the cost of a better existence is the loss of innocence about that very existence. The feeling of what happens is the answer to a question we never asked, and it is also the coin in a Faustian bargain that we could never have negotiated. Nature did it for us. (1999, 316)

Consciousness and Human Intentionality

THE NATURE of consciousness has occupied the thoughts of some of the most brilliant minds in philosophy, cognitive science, and psychology; and despite many claims to the contrary, it is still far from explained. John Searle states the issue as follows: " 'The problem of consciousness' is the problem of explaining exactly how neurobiological processes in the brain cause our subjective states of awareness or sentience; how exactly these states are realized in the brain structures; and how exactly consciousness functions in the overall economy of the brain and therefore how it functions in our life generally" (Searle 1997, 192). Controversy has raged, and still rages, over the issues in the first part of that description, but it is the final phrase—how it functions in our life generally—that is the focus here and that, strangely, appears to be relatively neglected as compared to the other issues. It is, however, at the very heart of all the issues involving human intentionality. To quote Searle (1997, 105) once more, "Darwin's greatest achievement was to show that the appearance of purpose, planning, teleology, and intentionality in the origin and development of human and animal species was entirely an illusion. The appearance could be explained by evolutionary processes that contained no such purposes at all. But the spread of ideas through imitation required the whole apparatus of human consciousness and intentionality."

Here I make no attempt at overall explanation but rather build on what we do know about consciousness to provide a foundation for understanding the process of change. Specifically we need to account for the extraordinary variety of human actions, ranging from the creativity of a Mozart or the genius of an Einstein, to the savagery of Attila the Hun (or Hitler, Stalin, or the Khmer Rouge), the religious fanaticism of Savonarola (an endless litany is available here), or the intolerance of dissent that has often characterized Catholics, Protestants, and Muslims both in the past and in the modern world. They are

CONSCIOUSNESS AND INTENTIONALITY

the complex product of the way consciousness interacts with the variety of human experiences, producing individuals with specific characteristics and beliefs and leading to broad patterns of societal behavior which have shaped and continue to shape economic change.

I

Consciousness is frequently divided into two levels, primary or core consciousness and higher order or extended consciousness.[1] The former is the state of being mentally aware of things in the world—of having mental images in the present. It is a characteristic of non-linguistic and non-semantic animals. Higher order or extended consciousness involves the recognition by a thinking subject of his or her actions or affections. It embodies a model of the personal, and of the past and future as well as the present. It exhibits direct awareness. We are conscious of being conscious. There are three aspects to a theory of consciousness:[2]

1. The physical assumption—the laws of physics are not violated. We do not need to evoke spirits or ghosts (although as we shall see humans do evoke spirits and ghosts in their explanation of phenomena).

2. The evolutionary assumption—consciousness arose as a phenotypic property at some time in the evolution of the species. The acquisition of consciousness either conferred evolutionary fitness directly on the individuals having it or provided the basis for other traits that enhanced fitness.

3. The Qualia (and most controversial) assumption—Qualia constitutes the collection of personal or subjective experiences, feelings, and sensations that accompany awareness and are unique to each individual.

Two features of consciousness deserve special emphasis: consciousness and emotions are not separable (Damasio 1999, 16); and consciousness and conscience are distinguishable: "consciousness pertains to the knowing of any object or action attributed to a self, while

---

[1] Much of this description and subsequent summary of the nature of consciousness is drawn from Edelman (1992) and Damasio (1999).

[2] See in particular Edelman (1992, Part III) for an elaboration of these issues.

conscience pertains to the good or evil to be found in actions or objects" (ibid., 27).

While some primates exhibit aspects of higher order consciousness, its development in human beings is the very foundation of human behavior and is intimately connected with the development of the human mind as described in chapter 3. That is, successive stages of human culture are grafted on to the genetic architecture to produce the complex structure we call consciousness. In particular the mythic stage, characterized by a shared narrative tradition built on language, and the final, theoretic stage of symbolically literate societies have moved consciousness in humans far beyond that of other primates. "Conscious human experience has given rise to culture, and culture to history. History is not simply a chronicle but an interpretation, encompassing suspected causes and values. Science has emerged within history, and it attempts to describe with considerably more certainty, the boundaries of the world—its constraints and its physical laws. But these laws cannot replace history or the actual course of individual lives" (Edelman 1992, 162). We may never completely untangle the complex interconnections between the genetic and cultural attributes, but combining the two enables us to make sense of the human condition over time even if some of the combinations are arbitrary assertions at this point. With that cautionary caveat let us see how far we can go in unraveling the complexities of human behavior.

Our story is one of the expansion of consciousness from its core beginnings common to other animals. There are two key features to this expansion that are central to this study. One is the imaginative development of explanations for the wider horizons of extended awareness that are embodied in superstitions, myths, dogmas, and religions. The second is the development of increasingly complex institutions and artifacts which reveal the intentionality of consciousness (Edelman 1992, 112) and regulate an ever expanding structure. We look at each in turn.

Extended awareness forces humans to confront and develop explanations for observable features of the environment not directly amenable to explanations that have evolved with learning about the immediate physical environment. "Higher order consciousness leads to a rich, cognitive, affective, and imaginative domain—feelings (qualia), thought, emotions, self-awareness, will, and imagination. It can construct artificial mental objects such as fantasies" (ibid., 198). Consciousness underlies non-rational and supernatural beliefs, which are a universal attribute of all human societies and would therefore appear to reflect innate qualities of the mind. Pascal Boyer maintains that the social inference system in the mind evolved to handle innate notions of morality and situations of misfortune. He describes some fundamental features common to all "supernatural explanations" as follows: "Our evolution as a species of cooperators is sufficient to explain the actual psychology of moral reasoning, the way children and adults represent moral dimensions of action. But then this requires no special concept of religious agent, no special code, no model to follow. However once you have concepts of supernatural agents with strategic information, these are made more salient and relevant by the fact that you can easily insert them in moral reasoning that would be there in any case. To some extent religious concepts are parasitic upon moral intuitions" (Boyer 2001, 191). Clearly there is a genetic origin to these explanations but to take us further it is necessary to explore the cultural conditioning that turns such explanations into driving forces in human development. *It is one thing to have supernatural explanations; it is something else to insist on conformity in beliefs about that supernatural explanation.* That takes us to the second feature.

Increasing self-awareness has led humans to ever more elaborate efforts to structure their environment as the development of language and then symbolic storage systems made possible far more complex forms of human organization. Edelman summarizes the issue as follows:

> Meaning takes shape in terms of concepts that depend on categorizations based on value. It grows with the history of remembered body sensations and mental images. The mixture of events is individual and, in large measure, unpredictable. When in society, linguistic and semantic capabilities arise and sentences involving metaphor are linked to thought, the capability to create new models of the world grows at an explosive rate. But one must remember that, because of its linkage to value and the concept of self, this system of meaning is almost never free of affect; it is charged with emotions. (1992, 170)

The widely varied experiences of humans in different settings have produced immensely varied cultures with different combinations of supernatural beliefs and institutions, but the important point is that it is the complex interplay between genetic predispositions and these varied experiences that gives us a starting point in understanding the process of societal change.

How do we account for cultural variation? Some evolutionary theorists have created a parallel category to genes to explain cultural evolution. They use the term memes to describe the intergenerational transfer of cultural attributes.[3] But such an extension is clearly misdirected. Cultural traits do not possess attributes parallel to those of genes and indeed the growing literature of the new institutional economics makes abundantly clear that institutions must be explained in terms of the intentionality of humans. Informal norms develop that blend the moral inference of genetic origin with the intentional aims of humans, which together provide the backbone of what we should mean by the term culture.

The powerful influence of myths, superstitions, and religions in shaping early societies came from their role in establishing order (the subject of chapter 8) and conformity. Ideological conformity to this day is a major force in reducing the costs of maintaining order, but it comes with the additional societal costs of preventing institutional change, punishing deviants, and serving as the source of endless human conflict with the clash of competing religions. Thus the expansion of consciousness is not only the source of the wonders of human creativity and the rich civilizations that humans have created but also a source of intolerance, prejudice, and human conflict. It could hardly be otherwise given its central role in human intentionality.

Conformity can be costly in a world of uncertainty. In the long run it produces stagnation and decay as humans confront ever new challenges in a non-ergodic world that requires innovative institutional creation because no one can know the right path to survival. Therefore, institutional diversity that allows for a range of choices is a superior survival trait, as Hayek has reminded us. Religious diversity

[3] This term was popularized by Richard Dawkins (1998, 302–8) and is featured in Dennett (1991). Searle (1997) devotes chapter 5 to a biting criticism of Dennett.

such as Luther and Calvin produced has long been celebrated as providing just such a stimulus, as Weber famously argued. But a more fundamental source of creativity has been the evolution of institutional diversity in general, of which Protestantism was one illustration and symptomatic of the overall diversity in thinking associated with the Renaissance. Political fragmentation in western Europe played just such a role in creating diverse and competing institutional settings for diverse beliefs and hence economic institutions which were critical in the relative rise of Europe as well as critical to the growth of impersonal exchange which underlies modern economic growth. All this is the subject of chapter 10.

II

If uncertainty is a constant in explaining institutional change, what difference does it make when the uncertainty changes from that associated with the physical environment to that associated with the human environment? All three of the sources of economic change—demography, stock of knowledge, and institutions—have been fundamentally altered. Population has grown at an unprecedented rate and the increase in human capital has been equally unprecedented. The growth of population has led to a world of ubiquitous externalities as humans were forced into ever closer proximity to each other, but in the additional context of the revolutionary changes in technology it has produced new social problems to be solved. The driving force in the development of the human environment has been the growth in the stock of knowledge which has revolutionized production technologies and provided the potential of a world of plenty. Equally it has created weapons of mass destruction capable of destroying us. The resultant institutional development has created more and more complex structures designed to deal with the consequent novel problems facing societies. Institutions as the incentive structure of societies have produced diverse inducements to invest in, expand, and apply this growing knowledge to solve problems of human scarcity.

The implications for consciousness have been that such inducements have expanded the human creative potential and in combination with diverse cultures produced widely varied responses to the novel problems confronting humans as a result of these changes. But the responses have not always been creative and productive. Sometimes the way experiences have interacted with consciousness has led to institutions that resulted in stagnation with resultant human frustration in the context of more dynamic societies. Problems posed by the transition of a belief system from one constructed to deal with the physical environment to one constructed to confront the complex problems of the human environment are at the core of the problems of economic development. There is nothing automatic about such a transition being successful.

Supernatural beliefs in general and organized religions in particular continue to play a critical role, but the change in the cultural context alters the nature of that role. The conflict between religious dogma and the growing knowledge of physical scientists from Copernicus and Galileo to Darwin has produced tensions in the Western world. In the rest of the world the widening gap in economic well-being created by differential incentives to invest and apply knowledge to solve economic problems has produced new fundamental conflicts. The failure of the Muslim world to continue its dynamic expansion after the twelfth century evidently reflected the rigidities that evolved in that culture in contrast to the dynamic changes in western Europe.[4] And in the modern world Muslim conformity in the context of an ever widening gap between the Muslim and Western world has at times hardened into fanaticism. No one needs to be reminded in the present world about the implications of religious fanaticism for conflict.

But if the driving force in the modern world is the growth in the stock of knowledge, we are left with the puzzle of the differential in its application leading to the ever widening gap between rich and poor countries—a difference which can only partially be explained by religious conformity. The controversies that rage about consciousness have focused on the body/mind connection to the relative neglect of its implications for shaping our lives. We seek to account for that complex mix of beliefs and institutions that evolve over time to determine the human condition.

[4] See Kuran (1997); see also Kuran (2003).

The marvelous achievements that come from the human mind require consciousness in the same fundamental way that they require life, and that life requires digestion and a balanced internal chemical milieu. But none of these marvelous achievements is directly caused by consciousness. They are instead a direct consequence of a nervous system which, being capable of consciousness, is also equipped with a vast memory, with the powerful ability to categorize items in memory, with the novel ability to code the entire spectrum of knowledge in language form, and with an enhanced ability to hold knowledge in mental display and manipulate it intelligently. Each of these abilities, in turn, can be traced to myriad mental and neural components. (Damasio 1999, 310–11)

A combination of "those states of sentience and awareness" that characterize consciousness and the evolving institutional framework is the source of that human condition. The diversity that we observe in the human condition over time, from the creative, imaginative developments of the Renaissance to the endless fanaticism, savagery, and warfare that is equally a part of our story, has at its source the way the mind acts on and reacts to the fundamental problems of a belief system attempting to make the transition from one constructed to deal with the physical environment to one capable of dealing with the human environment. We need to account for not only the macro issues of the fundamental sources of order and disorder in economies over time but also specific explanations of the diverse success of economies in dealing with novel problems that have confronted and continue to confront societies in a non-ergodic world. We can make some headway by reviewing empirical evidence on the nature of learning and human interaction in absorbing that learning in various social settings.

III

The place to begin such an explanation is with the genetic architecture that evolved in the several million years that humans evolved as hunters and gatherers. Innate cooperative behavior among small groups does appear to be a genetic trait and the previous chapter describes some work in experimental economics that provides empirical support for such a conclusion. But how far does such cooperation go beyond small groups and how does it modify the basic self-interest model underlying economic theory? Recent and current empirical research is beginning to give us some answers. Perhaps the most ambitious research undertaking arose in response to criticisms of the cultural uniformity of college students as the source of experimental studies. Accordingly a number of researchers (mostly anthropologists) who together had extensive experience in a variety of cultural settings each undertook an in-depth set of studies in the culture with which he or she was familiar using a common framework and research techniques. It is worth summarizing their results verbatim:

> First, the canonical model is not supported in any society studied. Second, there is more behavioral variability across groups than had been found in previous cross-cultural research, and the canonical model fails in a wider variety of ways than in previous experiments. Third, group level differences in economic organization and the degree of market integration explain a substantial portion of the behavioral variation across societies: the higher the degree of market integration and the higher the payoffs to cooperation, the greater the level of cooperation in experimental games. Fourth, individual-level economic and demographic variables do not explain behavior either within or across groups. Fifth, behavior in the experiments is generally consistent with economic patterns of everyday life in these societies.[5]

They conclude:

> While our results do not imply that economists should abandon the rational-actor framework, they do suggest two major revisions. First, the canonical model of the self-interested material payoff-maximizing actor is systematically violated. In all societies studied, [ultimatum game] offers are strictly positive and often substantially in excess of the expected income-maximizing offer, as are contributions in the public-goods game, while rejections of positive offers in some societies occur at a considerable rate. Second, preferences over economic choices are not exogenous as the canonical model would have it, but rather are shaped by the economic and social interactions of everyday life. This result implies that judgments in welfare

[5] "'Economic Man' in Cross-cultural Perspective: Behavioral Experiments in 15 Small-scale Societies," in Joseph Henrich et al. (2003).

economics that assume exogenous preferences are questionable, as are predictions of the effects of changing economic policies and institutions that
fail to take account of behavioral change. Finally, the connection between
experimental behavior and the structure of everyday economic life should
provide an important clue in revising the canonical model of individual
choice behavior. (Henrich et al. 2003, 39–40)

These conclusions are consistent with the arguments about learning
advanced in the previous chapter. It was argued that the learning
process appears to be a function of (1) the way in which a given
belief system filters the information derived from experiences, and (2)
the different experiences confronting individuals and societies at different times.

The social setting of the anthropologists' empirical research was a
world of uncertainty geared to the physical environment. Thus if we
are to account for the wide and still widening gap between rich and
poor countries we must explore the different experiences of societies
through time and the implications of these different experiences for the
development of different belief systems that produced widely different
abilities to confront the problems of the human environment. The research cited above, valuable as it is, only gives us a snapshot insight into
human behavior at particular moments of time; what we need is an in-
depth understanding of the incremental process of change through
time. The consciousness of humans and the consequent intentionality
that they displayed in the context of the stresses of evolving toward
more complex, interdependent cultures have produced the diverse institutional structures that in turn account for the varied differential
performance characteristics of societies. An increased understanding of
the process of change must integrate the rich details of human behavior
developed in the empirical work of anthropologists with the complex
belief systems that are a consequence of the complicated nature of self-
awareness resulting from consciousness.

The Scaffolds Humans Erect

ALL ORGANIZED ACTIVITY by humans entails a structure to define the "way the game is played," whether it is a sporting activity or the working of an economy. That structure is made up of institutions—formal rules, informal norms, and their enforcement characteristics. Take professional football. The game is played within a set of formal rules, informal norms (such as not deliberately injuring a key player on the opposing team), and the use of referees and umpires to enforce the rules and norms. How the game is actually played depends not only on the formal rules defining the incentive structure for the players and the strength of the informal norms but also on the effectiveness of enforcement of the rules. Changing the formal rules will alter the way the game is played but also, as anyone who has watched professional football knows, it frequently pays to evade the rules (and deliberately injure the quarterback of the opposing team). So it is with the performance characteristics of an economy. To understand performance we must explore in depth the way institutions "work," looking at both the consequences of formal incentives and the frequently unanticipated results.

The structure that humans create to order their political/economic environment is the basic determinant of the performance of an economy. It provides the incentives which shape the choices humans make. As with the team sport illustration, the strength of informal norms and the effectiveness of enforcement play a key part in the story. Where do the rules, informal norms, and for that matter the effectiveness of enforcement, come from? They are derived from the beliefs humans have.

The last chapter ended with a discussion of cognition in its cultural context, which determines the beliefs humans possess. This chapter explores the nature of that context broadly considered as a scaffolding that shapes human interaction. The scaffolds humans erect consist of physical capital and human capital, here considered in the broadest terms. That is, the physical capital is all the material artifacts that humans have accumulated and particularly the tools, techniques, and instruments they possess to control their environment; the human capital is the stock of knowledge humans possess as embodied in the beliefs they hold and the institutions they create reflecting those beliefs. While we are interested in the total character of the scaffolds (and indeed must integrate the broader aspects of the scaffolds in our specific analysis because they provide the specific context within which institutions evolve), this chapter focuses more narrowly on the institutional framework.

That institutional framework consists of the political structure that specifies the way we develop and aggregate political choices, the property rights structure that defines the formal economic incentives, and the social structure—norms and conventions—that defines the informal incentives in the economy. The institutional structure reflects the accumulated beliefs of the society over time, and change in the institutional framework is usually an incremental process reflecting the constraints that the past imposes on the present and the future. All this—and more—makes up the structure that humans erect to deal with the human landscape. Successively we shall consider the relationship between beliefs and institutions, the cultural heritage and its implications for path dependence, the structure of decision making that aggregates and implements choices, and finally the nature of institutional change.[1]

I

There is an intimate relationship between belief systems and the institutional framework. Belief systems embody the internal representation of the human landscape. Institutions are the structure that humans impose on that landscape in order to produce the desired outcome. Belief systems therefore are the internal representation and institutions the external manifestation of that representation. Thus the structure of an

---

[1] I shall not repeat here the analysis of institutions I have developed in earlier studies. This study does build on the earlier work, extending and in some instances modifying earlier analysis.

economic market reflects the beliefs of those in a position to make the rules of the game, who enact rules that will produce the outcomes (that is, the sort of market) they desire, whether those desires are to create monopoly or to create a competitive market (always with the caveat that their beliefs may be incorrect and produce unanticipated consequences). When conflicting beliefs exist, the institutions will reflect the beliefs of those (past as well as present) in a position to effect their choices, a subject to be explored in the following paragraphs.

The intimate interrelationship of beliefs and institutions, while evident in the formal rules of a society, is most clearly articulated in the informal institutions—norms, conventions, and internally held codes of conduct. These informal institutions not only embody the moral codes of the belief system, which tend to have common characteristics across cultures, but also embody the norms particular to individual societies, which are very diverse across cultures. While formal institutions can be changed by fiat, informal institutions evolve in ways that are still far from completely understood and therefore are not typically amenable to deliberate human manipulation.[2]

II

As noted earlier, culture consists of the intergenerational transfer of norms, values, and ideas. But the role of culture we are concerned with here is described by Hutchins and Hazelhurst as "a process that permits the learning of prior generations to have more direct effect on the learning of subsequent generations" (1992, 690). Thus they speculate that a population over many generations could be capable of discovering things that no individual could learn in a lifetime (ibid., 690). That which was transmitted and put in place by past generations is described by them as the artifactual structure. This artifactual structure is the learning of past generations transmitted as culture into the belief structure of present generations. While the formal rules a society puts in place will reflect this heritage, the informal constraints embodied in

[2] There is now an immense—and growing—literature on norms. A good summary from an evolutionary perspective is Bendor and Swistak (2001).

norms of behavior, conventions, and self-imposed codes of conduct are the most important "carrier" of the artifactual structure. Formal rules can be changed overnight (by a revolution for example); informal constraints change much more slowly and play a critical role in the evolution of polities. "Local learning" is derived from the specific environment (both physical and intellectual) of a society. As changes occur in that environment they are gradually assimilated into the socio-cultural linguistic inheritance and embodied in the artifactual structure.

Hayek maintained that culture is "the transmission in time of our accumulated stock of knowledge" (Hayek 1960, 27). He included in knowledge all the human adaptations to the environment which were derived from past experience—habits, skills, emotional attitudes, as well as institutions. Hayek's theory of cultural evolution largely involved a spontaneous process since he believed the ability of human beings to comprehend the ever more complex structure of human interaction was limited. But human intentionality is not spontaneous. Humans deliberately try to shape their future and indeed have no alternative but to try to structure human interaction—the alternative is anarchy or chaos. However imperfectly they are bound to do it, they have no choice. The issue is how they do it.[3]

How human societies attempt to shape their future leads us to deal directly with a fundamental aspect of the process of change—its historical nature. We cannot understand where we are going without an understanding of where we have been. How the past connects with the present and future is the subject of path dependence—a term which is used, misused, and abused. It could mean nothing more than that choices in the present are constrained by the heritage of institutions accumulated from the past. But if that were all there was to path dependence then we could undertake radical change when we observed that the institutions were performing badly. A step toward a more comprehensive understanding of the term is to recognize that the institutions that have accumulated give rise to organizations whose survival depends on the perpetuation of those institutions and which hence will devote resources to preventing any alteration that threatens their sur-

---

[3] Viktor Vanberg (1994) has an excellent summary of Hayek's theory as well as trenchant criticisms of some of his normative conclusions.

vival. A great deal of path dependence can be usefully understood in that context. The previous chapter suggests a still more complex view of path dependence. The interaction of beliefs, institutions, and organizations in the total artifactual structure makes path dependence a fundamental factor in the continuity of a society (a subject to be explored in more depth in part II). Path dependence is not "inertia," rather it is the constraints on the choice set in the present that are derived from historical experiences of the past. Understanding the process of change entails confronting directly the nature of path dependence in order to determine the nature of the limits to change that it imposes in various settings.

III

The scaffolds humans erect not only define the economic and political game but also determine who will have access to the decision-making process. They further define the formal structure of incentives and disincentives that are a first approximation to the choice set. But the scaffold is much more. It is equally the informal structure of norms, conventions, and codes of conduct. And still beyond that it is the way the institutional structure acts upon and reacts to other factors that affect both the demographic characteristics of a society and changes in the stock of knowledge.

The formal institutional structure of a society consists of the constitutional framework broadly conceived—that is, the structure that defines the way the political and economic game is intended to be played. While an examination of the U.S. Constitution would give us some understanding of the decision-making process in the United States, it would be so incomplete as to be of limited value. How the game is actually played is a consequence of the formal structure, the informal institutional constraints, and the enforcement characteristics. In a paper for the World Bank, Cox and McCubbins (2001, 2–3) summarize the formal structure of a representative society as follows:

> The structure of a polity may be described as a sequence of principal-agent relationships. In a typical representative democracy, for example, there are three broad delegations that might be noted. First, the sovereign people

delegate decision-making power (usually via a written constitution) to a national legislature and executive. The primary tools that the people retain in order to ensure appropriate behavior on the part of their representatives are two: the power to replace them at election time; and the power to set the constitutional rules of the political game. . . . A second step in the delegation of power occurs when the details of the internal organization of the legislature and executive are settled. . . . A third step in the delegation of power takes the legislature (or its political chiefs) as principal and various bureaus and agencies as agents. . . . It is our argument here that the structure of these principal-agent relationships determines, in large measure, the choice of public policy.

But the implications for performance of this structure can be most clearly illuminated by a transaction cost approach to politics. The conception of transaction costs as the costs entailed in the measurement and enforcement of agreements can be usefully applied to analyzing the efficiency of political markets. For example, the U.S. Congress has relatively low-cost transacting as a result of an elaborate institutional structure that facilitates exchanges over time and makes possible credible commitment.[4] But while the institutional structure has made possible relatively low-cost exchange, this consequence does not mean that the overall political market is efficient. Highlighting the inherent problems of political markets through an exploration of a hypothetical political market with zero transaction costs will put the issues in sharp focus.[5]

Such a political market would be one in which constituents could accurately evaluate the policies pursued by competing candidates in terms of the net effect on their well-being; only legislation (or regulation) that maximized the aggregate income of the affected parties to the exchange would be enacted; and compensation to those adversely affected would ensure that no party was injured by the action. To achieve such results, constituents and legislators would need to possess true models that allowed them to accurately evaluate the gains and losses of alternative policies, legislators would have to vote the constit-

---

[4] See Weingast and Marshall (1988) for an analysis of the organization of Congress in these terms.

[5] The following paragraphs are drawn from North (1990a).

uents' interests—that is, the vote of each legislator would be weighed by the net gains and losses of the constituents, and losers would be compensated such as to make the exchange worthwhile to them. It is possible that the intermediate steps by the legislator—voting what he or she perceives as the constituents' interest and having the votes crudely weighted by the perceived net gain or loss to the constituents—are approximated by the complex legislative structure. But beyond that there are several questions. First, how does the constituent know his/her interests? What will the competing candidates really do? Not even the candidates know the variety of issues they will be called on to legislate that will directly or indirectly affect the constituents' welfare. And even if they did, they would have to know the effect on constituents' welfare—easy, perhaps, in cases of obvious redistribution or bills directly influencing income and employment in a district, but simply unknowable for a large proportion of the bills. And as for the constituent, he or she would have to know the consequences of the multitude of bills enacted by the representative and the effect on the individual's pocket book.

Further, how well does the institutional structure of the legislature approximate the zero transaction cost model? The U.S. Congress has relatively low-cost transacting and as compared to a totalitarian regime is clearly efficient; but as the endless studies of the U.S. Congress attest, a very mixed set of incentive signals provide for strategic voting and pork barrel legislation.

And how close are intentions to outcomes? The models that guide legislators are one source of error. Legislators simply do not possess the information or theoretical models to achieve the desired results. More than that, legislation is enacted and implemented by agents who have their own utility which will affect the final outcomes.

Imperfect models of the complex environment that the politician (and constituent) is attempting to order, institutional inability to get credible commitment between principal and agent (voter and legislator, legislator and policy implementer), the high cost of information, and the negligible payoff to the individual constituent of acquiring information all conspire to make political markets inherently imperfect.[6] Surely

---

[6] For more sanguine views about the efficiency of political markets see Lupia, McCubbins, and Popkin (1999).

this conclusion should not be surprising. After all, the basic separation between the polity and the economy has always, even among confirmed libertarians, left a residual of activities to be undertaken by government because of the inherent difficulty that arose from the public good attributes, free riding, and costly (and asymmetric) information of certain types of activities. We do not expect a random sample of issues to become public. Those that can be handled readily by individual or small group bargaining do not need to be placed on the public agenda. What remains for the public agenda are issues with attributes described above, or those the market outcome of which some groups do not like—groups who have enhanced bargaining power in the polity to achieve their objectives. Bargaining strength and the incidence of transaction costs are not the same in the polity as in the economy, otherwise it would not be worthwhile for groups to shift the issues to the political arena. Thus the selection process is one in which the high transaction cost items gravitate to the polity. Madison's insightful views about the inherent nature of the political process as described in *Federalist Paper* no. 10—in effect he maintained that polities tend to be captured by special interests and used by them for their own advantage at the expense of the general public and that this was a universal dilemma of polities throughout history—are as pertinent today as they were two centuries ago.

The previous paragraphs have schematically outlined the political framework of representative government, a subject that has been explored at length by political scientists. It is more difficult to model the political process in third world polities where corruption, bribery, and Mafia-like extortion tend to be the order of the day. Modeling the actual structure as it in fact works in such polities has increasingly occupied the attention of political economists in recent years, but we are some distance from having good working models. The enormous diversity of performance of polities makes the subject a crucial one for improving our understanding of economic change.[7]

---

[7] The literature on the subject is growing. The Cambridge series on *The Political Economy of Institutions and Decisions* contains some of the most important work on the subject. A pioneering study of the role of the polity in American economic development was Hughes (1977).

In general, then, we have been less successful in modeling the political process than in modeling economic markets. The brief account of transacting in political markets suggests some of the reasons. Political markets do not work like economic markets. The difficulty begins with the behavioral assumptions we employ. They are more complicated than those we employ in economic models, reflecting moral and ethical norms and "non-rational" behavioral responses. Political decisions make more complicated demands on cognition because of the nature of consciousness and intentionality. The complex blend of "rational self-interested behavior" (the foundation of economic models) with ideological beliefs stemming from the self-awareness of humans poses a major challenge to political scientists. And it is precisely in this context that the political market in its dynamic context offers the promise of more effectively dealing with uncertainty in a non-ergodic world. As described in chapter 2, uncertainty can be reduced by institutions that encourage an open-ended process of discovery. Democracy in its ideal form does precisely that. Michael Wohlgemuth (2003) in his essay "Democracy as an Evolutionary Method" states three propositions that characterize the dynamic aspects of democracy:

1. Political preferences and opinions build on fallible conjectures and theories.

2. Democratic opinion-formation results from an open-ended process of interactive learning and discovery.

3. The important element in this process is not the supremacy, but the contestability of current majority opinions.

Wohlgemuth's approach is derived from Hayek (1960, 108ff.), who argued that "Democracy is above all, a process of forming opinion. . . . It is in its dynamic, rather than in its static, aspects that the value of democracy proves itself. . . . The ideal of democracy rests on the belief that the view which will direct government emerges from an independent and spontaneous process. It requires, therefore, the existence of a large sphere independent of majority control in which the opinions of the individuals are formed."

This positive view of the crucial role of democracy in both the perpetuation of liberty and the promotion of economic growth is the very foundation of liberal (in the classic meaning of the term) thought. But such a view poses a conundrum. When we run regressions between democracy and economic growth the results are positive but very weak (Barro 1996). I shall attempt to confront this conundrum in Part II of this study; here I simply set out the analytical framework.

It is the polity that defines and enforces the formal economic rules of the game and therefore is the primary source of economic performance. The formal economic rules are broadly speaking property rights defining ownership, use, rights to income, and alienability of resources and assets as expressed in laws and regulations. There is an immense literature on this subject;[8] there is less on the way informal constraints influence economic performance. We do have a good deal of recent research modeling specific norms and their impact set in a game theoretic framework, but examining the overall consequences of culture for economic performance is still in its infancy. Demsetz (1967) makes the point that a norm may emerge when an activity creates rising external effects and the norm has the consequence of internalizing those effects. I have argued (North 1990b) that in societies where interaction is on a small and personal level informal norms generally suffice and will only get converted into formal rules as impersonal exchange and the necessary growing use of external symbolic storage systems in such complex human environments induce such changes. But we still have a way to go to deal with the origins of norms and the persistence of inefficient norms. I start with the issue of origins.

Any discussion of the role of beliefs and values in shaping change inevitably turns to Max Weber's pioneering work. His *Protestant Ethic and the Spirit of Capitalism* emphasizes the religious origins of such values. Yujiro Hayami has stressed the importance of moral codes in business transactions in Japan. "it was an admixture of Confucianism, Buddhism and Shintoism, but in substance it taught the same morals that Adam Smith considered to be the basis of the wealth of nations—frugality, industry, honesty and fidelity. Clearly this ideology was an important support for commercial and industrial development in the

[8] An excellent discussion is in Barzel (1997).

late Tokugawa period, as it suppressed moral hazards and reduced the costs of market transactions" (Hayami and Aoki 1998, 15).

With Jean-Philippe Platteau, Hayami (1998) turned to a different origin of social norms. The two emphasized the contrast between redistributive norms in African tribal communities and the reciprocal norms in Asian village communities and ascribed the differences to different degrees of settlement density and consequent property rights in agriculture. "Culturally, people whose living is based on settled agriculture are the believers of 'great religions' e.g., Buddhism in Thailand, Islam in Indonesia, Christianity in the Philippines, Buddhism and Confucianism in China, Korea and Japan" (ibid., 386). The implication of their analysis is that the religions derive from the basic demographic conditions rather than being the independent variable initiating the resultant norms. They want to draw attention to "structural forces that are at the root of serious market imperfections, to wrong incentive systems that arise from traditional social fabrics (and not from government policy mistakes) and to natural or technological handicaps, all outcomes which tend to make agricultural progress especially costly or difficult to achieve in SSA [Sub-Saharan Africa]" (ibid., 359). Platteau and Hayami have an important point in their emphasis on population density and land-use patterns as important in the African/Asian contrast and their essay suggests the origins of a variety of norms important in Asian development. But despite a voluminous literature on this subject we are some distance from a definitive understanding of the source and implications of diverse cultural backgrounds.

Even more troubling for good performance is the persistence of inefficient norms. Thrainn Eggertsson (1996, 1998) has documented the persistence of such norms in Iceland, where for centuries the people maintained norms that prevented them from exploiting the rich fishery resources at their doorstep. Jan Elster (1989) has written extensively about such norms. But again, our understanding of such issues is incomplete.

The foregoing discussion should make clear the way the formal and informal institutions and their enforcement characteristics determine the efficiency of economic organization and (hence jointly with production costs) economic efficiency. Transaction costs enable us to measure the costs of exchange and give us a tool both to analyze the costs of economic organization and to get a better understanding of sources of poor economic performance.[9]

IV

How do institutions themselves change? Five propositions about institutional change are[10]

1. The continuous interaction between institutions and organizations in the economic setting of scarcity and hence competition is the key to institutional change.

2. Competition forces organizations to continually invest in skills and knowledge to survive. The kinds of skills and knowledge individuals and their organizations acquire will shape evolving perceptions about opportunities and hence choices that will incrementally alter institutions.

3. The institutional framework provides the incentives that dictate the kinds of skills and knowledge perceived to have the maximum pay-off.

4. Perceptions are derived from the mental constructs of the players.

5. The economies of scope, complementarities, and network externalities of an institutional matrix make institutional change overwhelmingly incremental and path dependent.

Each of these propositions deserves elaboration.

1. The study of institutions and institutional change necessitates as a first requirement the conceptual separation of institutions from organizations. Institutions are the rules of the game, organizations are the players; it is the interaction between the two that shapes institutional change (see North 1990b for an elaboration of this distinction).

Institutions are the constraints that human beings impose on human interaction. Those constraints (together with the standard constraints of economics) define the opportunity set in the economy. Organizations consist of groups of individuals bound together by some common

[9] For an overview as applied to the firm see Williamson and Masten (1999).
[10] This section is drawn from North (1995a).

objectives. Firms, trade unions, cooperatives are examples of economic organizations; political parties, the Senate, regulatory agencies illustrate political organizations; religious bodies, clubs are examples of social organizations. The opportunities provided by the institutional matrix determine the kinds of organizations that will come into existence; the entrepreneurs of organizations induce institutional change as they face the ubiquitous competition derived from an economic world of scarcity. As they perceive new or altered opportunities they induce institutional change by altering the rules (either directly by political bodies or indirectly by economic or social organizations pressuring political organizations); or by deliberately (and sometimes accidentally) altering the kinds and effectiveness of enforcement of rules or the effectiveness of sanctions and other means of informal constraint enforcement. Historically, as organizations in the course of interaction evolve new informal means of exchange, social norms, conventions, and codes of conduct may wither away.

2. New or altered opportunities may be a result of exogenous changes in the external environment which alter relative prices to organizations; or they may be a consequence of endogenous competition among the organizations of the polity and the economy that induce the growth of knowledge and hence innovations. In either case the ubiquity of competition in the overall economic setting of scarcity induces entrepreneurs and the members of their organizations to invest in skills and knowledge. Whether it is learning by doing on the job or the acquisition of formal knowledge, the key to survival is improving the efficiency of the organization relative to that of rivals.

While idle curiosity surely is an innate source of acquiring knowledge among human beings, the rate of accumulating knowledge is clearly tied to the pay-offs. Secure monopolies (such as U.S. public school systems), be they organizations in the polity or ones in the economy, simply do not have to improve to survive. But firms, political parties, or even institutions of higher learning faced with rival organizations must strive to improve their efficiency. When competition is "muted" (for whatever reasons) organizations will have little incentive to invest in new knowledge and in consequence will not induce rapid institutional change. Stable institutional structures will be the result. Vigorous organizational competition will produce rapid institutional change.

3. There is no implication in the foregoing proposition of evolutionary progress or economic growth—only of change. The institutional matrix defines the opportunity set, be it one that makes the highest pay-offs in an economy income redistribution or one that provides the highest pay-offs to productive activity. While every economy provides a mixed set of incentives for both types of activity, the relative weights are crucial factors in its performance. The organizations that come into existence will reflect the pay-off structure. More than that, the direction of their investment in skills and knowledge will equally reflect the underlying incentive structure. If the highest rate of return in an economy is to piracy we can expect that the organizations will invest in skills and knowledge that will make them better pirates. Similarly, if there are high returns to productive activities we will expect organizations to devote resources to investing in skill and knowledge that will increase productivity.

The immediate investment of economic organizations in vocational and on-the-job training obviously will depend on the perceived benefits. Much more fundamental, the extent to which societies will invest in formal education, schooling, the dissemination of knowledge, and both applied and pure research will mirror the perceptions of the entrepreneurs of political and economic organizations. In similar fashion, the institutional matrix will embody incentives with respect to fertility behavior and by the way in which the incentives influence knowledge about sanitation and infectious diseases, they may effect control over sources of morbidity and mortality. But it is important to stress that the institutions put in place will reflect the beliefs of the players, which in the case of fertility and mortality sources have been notoriously wrong throughout much of history.[11]

4. The key to the choices that individuals make is their perceptions: that is the way the mind interprets the information it receives. As noted in previous chapters, the mental constructs individuals form to explain and interpret the world around them are partly a result of their cultural heritage, partly a result of the "local" everyday problems they confront and must solve, and partly a result of non-local learning. The mix between these sources in interpreting one's environment obviously varies

[11] See Easterlin (1996) and David (1997) for fascinating illustrations.

as between for example a Papuan tribesman on the one hand and an economist in the United States on the other (although there is no implication that the latter's perceptions are independent of his or her cultural heritage).

Individuals from different backgrounds will interpret the same evidence differently and in consequence make different choices. If the information feedback on the consequences of choices was "complete" then individuals with the same utility function would gradually correct their perceptions and over time converge to a common equilibrium; but as emphasized in chapter 2 imperfect comprehension together with a non-ergodic world in continuous change provides assurance that we can, and will, get it wrong very frequently. As Frank Hahn has succinctly put it, "There is a continuum of theories that agents can hold and act upon without ever encountering events which lead them to change their theories" (1987, 324). The result is that multiple equilibria are possible/prevalent.

5. The viability, profitability, and indeed survival of the organizations of a society typically depend on the existing institutional matrix. That institutional structure has brought them into existence and upon it their complex web of interdependent contracts and other relationships has been constructed. Two implications follow. Institutional change is typically incremental and is path dependent.

It is incremental because large-scale change will create too many opponents among existing organizations that will be harmed and therefore oppose such change. Revolutionary change will only occur in the case of gridlock among competing organizations which thwarts the ability of organizations to capture gains from trade. Path dependence will occur because the direction of the incremental institutional change will be broadly consistent with the existing institutional matrix (for the reasons described above) and will be governed by the kinds of knowledge and skills that the entrepreneurs and members of organizations have invested in.

Now let me amplify each of the propositions.

Proposition 1: The study of institutions has been bedeviled by ambiguity about the meaning of the term. Institutions are the rules of the game; organizations are the players. They entail different modelings to understand the way they operate and interact with each other. Modeling institutions is modeling the man-made constraints on human interaction that define the incentive structure of the society. Modeling organizations is theorizing about the structure, governance, and policies of purposive social entities.[12]

While individuals are the actors it is typically individuals in their capacities as part of organizations that make the decisions that alter the rules of the game.

Proposition 2 simply restates the fundamental postulate of economics and specifically applies it to the organizations of an economy. It bears emphasizing, however, that the stock of knowledge the individuals in a society possess is the deep underlying determinant of the performance of economies and societies and changes in that stock of knowledge is the key to the evolution of economies. The rise of the Western world was ultimately a consequence of the kinds of skills and knowledge (not only "productive knowledge" but notably knowledge about military technology) that were deemed valuable to the political and economic organizations of the medieval Western world. The key point is that learning by individuals and organizations is the major influence on the evolution of institutions.

Proposition 3: Throughout most of history and indeed in much of the present world economies have been perceived by the players as zero sum games in which the acquisition of skills and knowledge has as its objective doing better at the expense of others. The institutional matrix has reflected the bargaining strength of those able to make or change the rules. Their perceptions with respect to the gains to be made by redistributive versus productive activities will shape the rules of the game and the resultant opportunity set. That in turn will shape perceptions about the kinds of skills and knowledge that will pay off. The transition from a belief system built to deal with the uncertainties of the physical environment to one confronting the opportunities of the human environment involves a change in perceptions from a zero sum

[12] There is an extensive literature modeling the internal structure of organizations, notably by Oliver Williamson, Gary Miller, and Jim March (among many others). This literature is invaluable in understanding how decision making occurs inside organizations. It is not the focus of this study, which explores the interaction between institutions and organizations.

game to a positive sum game and is a critical turning point in the process of economic change.

Proposition 4: Where do the perceptions that individuals possess come from? Neo-classical theory simply skips this step under the assumption that people know what they are doing. This may be true in evaluating opportunity costs at the supermarket, but it is wildly incorrect when it comes to making more complicated choices in a world of incomplete information and of subjective models used to interpret that incomplete information.

What we mean by rationality requires explicit specification for social scientists in general but particularly for those who employ rational choice models. If we are going to employ the choice theoretic approach we must be explicit about just how people arrive at the choices they make. Being explicit entails specification of the subjective models people possess to interpret information and of the information they receive.

Proposition 5: Why can't economies reverse their direction overnight? This is surely a puzzle in a world that operated as neo-classical theory would have us believe. But it is simply a fact that the overwhelming majority of change is incremental, gradual, and constrained by the historical past. Incorporating the implications of the above analysis and description of institutional change provides us with the basic building blocks we need in order to explore the overall nature of the process of economic change.

This characterization of institutional change is a major building block in our construction of an understanding of the process of economic change.

Taking Stock

LET US SEE if we can put together where we are so far in our understanding of the process of economic change. What do we know and what do we need to know to make further progress? We have accumulated a great deal of evidence on the performance of economies over time and we know a good deal about the underlying sources of productivity increase which is the source of improved economic performance. What is still missing is a body of theory that will integrate the analysis of institutional change developed in the previous chapter into the larger context of an overall understanding of the process of economic change.

Neo-classical economic theory provides an understanding of the operation of markets in developed economies but was never intended to explain how markets and overall economies evolved. It has three fundamental deficiencies which must be overcome to understand the process of economic change. It is frictionless, it is static, and it does not take into account human intentionality. By frictionless I mean that markets function without any "outside" intervention and in consequence no resources are devoted to the process of exchange (transaction costs are zero), and by static I mean that the dimension of time is not involved in the analysis; intentionality requires an understanding of the way humans make choices.

Evolutionary theory which is explicitly concerned with time was inspired by Darwin's path-breaking studies and has intrigued economists from Veblen to Marshall but it is only in recent years that it has inspired systematic work in the social sciences. Since a striking feature of the mental equipment of humans is the ability to engage in representational redescription, it was natural to derive inspiration from evolutionary theory. There is a rich literature applying evolutionary concepts taken from biology to economics.[1] It would take us too far afield to explore

[1] For recent surveys see Witt (1992); Hodgson (1993); and Denzau and Zak (2001).

the controversies that swirl around evolutionary biology and the extensions to human evolution.[2] This study has certainly drawn inspiration from this literature but it is important to emphasize two significant distinctions between biological and economic evolution.[3] In the former variation occurs through mutation and sexual recombination along Mendelian lines. There is no close analogy in economic evolution.[4] And as stressed earlier, the selection mechanisms in evolutionary theory are not informed by beliefs about the eventual consequences as they are in economic evolution. And indeed in the latter it is the intentionality of the players as expressed through the institutions they create which shapes performance.

To overcome the deficiencies of both neo-classical theory and evolutionary theory we must confront the issues of frictionless economies, of time, and of human intentionality. In succeeding sections of this chapter I shall do just that, summarizing both what we have learned and what we must learn to understand the process of economic change. We can then set these issues within the overall context of the problems of societal change.

I

It is institutional analysis, of course, that addresses the issues of frictionless economies, and substantial progress has been made in the past several decades in exploring the issues, much of which is summarized in chapter 5. Institutions structure human interaction by providing an incentive structure to guide human behavior. But an incentive structure requires a theory of the way the mind perceives the world and its functioning so that the institutions will provide those incentives. Different experiences of societies through time will produce different perceptions of the way the world works and therefore require different institutions to provide the same incentives. It is necessary to understand the way

---

[2] For example, for an unsparing critique of Stephen Jay Gould and Stuart Kauffman see Dawkins (1998).

[3] An early source of inspiration was Boyd and Richerson (1985).

[4] See Dawkins (1998) and Dennett (1995) for illustrations.

learning takes place in different environments and the consequences in terms of belief systems and resultant institutions.

But even within a given belief system institutions are always imperfect incentive systems. Formal rules, informal constraints, and enforcement characteristics vary in the degree to which they shape behavior. The key to useful institutional analysis is to take into account the imperfect nature of institutional incentive systems and build that understanding into the analytical framework. Only then will the institutional analysis make the essential contribution to political economic analysis that it is capable of making. Take the case of political institutions.

To put it bluntly we know a lot about polities but not how to fix them.[5] We do not have any clear understanding of "what makes polities work" in the same sense that we do about how economic markets work. The transaction cost comparisons described in chapter 5 highlight the differences and point to our lack of understanding. Does democracy provide the ideal setting for economic growth, or is an authoritarian regime more conducive to favorable societal change? Taiwan and South Korea both jumpstarted growth with authoritarian regimes before becoming democratic, and Singapore as of this writing remains an authoritarian state with an impressive performance. Certainly an authoritarian ruler bent on promoting growth has a freer hand than a democracy beset by multiple political and economic interests.

The dilemma is a straightforward one. The government is not a disinterested party in the economy. By the very nature of the political process briefly described earlier, the government has strong incentives to behave opportunistically to maximize the rents of those with access to the government decision-making process. In some cases this means that the government is, in effect, a kleptocracy; in other cases it means that the government will cartelize economic activity in favor of politically influential parties. In rare cases the government designs and enforces a set of rules of the game that encourage productive activity.

[5] As, until recently, co-editor of the Cambridge University Press series on *The Political Economy of Institutions and Decisions*, I have been impressed by the growth of our academic understanding over a substantial range of issues; and as someone who has "played God" in attempting to improve performance of transition and third world economies I have been made acutely aware of the shortcomings in our understanding

Analysis in previous chapters has stressed the imperfect understanding humans possess of their environment, the consequent subjective belief systems that they possess, and the transaction costs of polities. Political markets are inherently less efficient than economic markets. And "inefficient" here means that the formal and informal institutions only very imperfectly embody the implied incentive structure. Indeed if we wish to explain the relative success of polities like that of the United States over the past several centuries we must turn to the critical role that informal constraints in combination with the formal rules played in that story. Formal models of polities which incorporate the behavioral assumptions of economists confront the fundamental dilemma that a polity (in which the players operate on the basis of rational self-interest) that is strong enough to specify and enforce economic rules of the game is strong enough to allow factions (to use Madison's felicitous term) to use the polity to pursue their own narrow self-interests at the expense of the general welfare. The elusive key to improved political ordering is the creation of credible commitment on the part of the players. While Madison's checks and balances take us part way to resolving this problem it requires, in addition, informal constraints that will redirect behavior to produce more felicitous outcomes.

Improving the predictive ability of institutions as incentive structures entails more detailed empirical research on the performance characteristics of institutions in various settings. We are making headway in getting a better understanding of the performance characteristics of institutions in various settings but much more empirical research is needed before we can begin to develop more generalizations about institutions.

II

Time involves the interaction between experiences and learning and by the very nature of the learning process imposes limits on human foresight and therefore on any theory of dynamic change. Indeed such a theory would have to so simplify the complex process of human inter-

---

of how to set them right which means in the first instance creating a political-economic structure that will lead to an improvement in their performance.

action that it would have limited usefulness. That is not to say that evolutionary game theory built on learning and imitation as driving forces cannot be a useful tool of analysis. Avner Greif (forthcoming a) not only uses game theory imaginatively to give us a richer understanding of equilibrium situations but also explores the stability of such equilibria with the purpose of giving us insight into the transition from one equilibrium to another. But there still are limits on human foresight that are a consequence of the two fundamental limitations: (1) we cannot know today what we will learn tomorrow which will shape our tomorrow's actions and (2) it is a non-ergodic world.

These limitations do not quarrel with the knowledge we have gained on improving our chances of solving problems of a non-ergodic world. Our task is to explain the diverse belief systems that have evolved historically and in the present, which have very different implications for structure, organization, and economic success of societies. The focus is on the interaction between the mind and the external environment. What kind of learning do the individuals in a society acquire through time? Time in this context embodies not only current experiences but the cumulative experiences of past generations embodied in the culture of a society. "Culture can literally reconfigure the use patterns of the brain; and it is probably a safe inference from our current knowledge of cerebral plasticity that those patterns of use determine much about how the exceptionally plastic human central nervous system is ultimately organized, in terms of cognitive structure" (Donald 1991, 14). Learning then is an incremental process filtered by the culture of a society which determines the perceived pay-offs. As discussed in chapter 4, the learning process appears to be a function of the way in which a given belief system filters the information derived from experiences; and of the different experiences confronting individuals and societies at different times. Successful economic development will occur when the belief system that has evolved has created a "favorable" artifactual structure that can confront the novel experiences that the individual and society face and resolve positively the novel dilemmas. Failures will occur when the novel experiences are so far removed from the artifactual structure of the evolved belief system that individual and society do not have the "building blocks" of the mind and artifactual structure to resolve the novel problems. If we are going to come to grips with an understanding of the differential performance of different parts of the world both over time and cross-sectionally in the modern world it is here that we must begin. Put simply the richer the artifactual structure the more likely are we to confront novel problems successfully. That is what is meant by adaptive efficiency; creating the necessary artifactual structure is an essential goal of economic policy.

III

The rational choice models of economists involve human intentionality and have been valuable in modeling human behavior in particular contexts. But as discussed in chapters 3 and 4, they have not confronted the problems of human behavior we must explain even in the restrictive domain of market analysis. Brian Arthur has characterized those problems very well as follows: "Economic agents, be they banks, consumers, firms, or investors continually adjust their market moves, buying decisions, prices, and forecasts to the situations these moves or decisions or prices or forecasts together create. But unlike ions in a spin glass, which always react in a simple way to their local magnetic field, economic elements (human agents) react with strategy and foresight by considering outcomes that might result as a consequence of behavior they might undertake" (Arthur 1992, 108). This adds a layer of complication to economics that is not experienced in the natural sciences. The direction of research of Arthur and others at the Santa Fe Institute is complexity theory, which is "not an adjunct to standard economic theory but theory at a more general, out-of-equilibrium level" (ibid.). It employs high powered mathematics and draws its inspiration from non-linear dynamics. The verdict is still out on just how far this approach takes us.[6]

But our concern is more than explaining behavior in well-developed markets. Indeed a central concern is with the way the mind interacts with the external environment in different contexts and specifically in markets characterized by personal exchange. Why personal exchange?

[6] For a survey of the progress so far, see Arthur, Durlauf, and Lane (1997). I have an essay in this volume dealing with the process of long run economic change.

Because innate characteristics of human behavior derived from millions of years of human interaction in a setting of hunter/gatherer societies produced genetic predispositions that are the starting place to explore human behavior. The ongoing research by a group of anthropologists briefly discussed in chapter 4 does explore human behavior in a variety of cultural settings ranging from hunter/gatherer societies to relatively "developed" societies. The questions for which we require answers are what kinds of political, social, and economic organization characterized a world of personalized exchange which dominated societies where the uncertainties were those from the physical environment and then what are the consequences as humans attempt to make the transition to one where the uncertainties arise from the human environment. Personal exchange by its very nature restricts the range of economic activity to clientism and repeated face-to-face interaction. Impersonal exchange entails a host of political, social, and economic institutions that "violate" the innate genetic predispositions that evolved in the several million years of hunter/gather environments. Both successful market exchange and political democracy hang on our ability to deal with these issues.

IV

In building a new framework that will take into account the limitations of current theory to provide a better understanding of the process of economic change we must deal with a number of problems that have their sources in the foregoing discussion.

Humans start out with genetic features which provide the initial architecture of the mind; the mind interacts with the cultural heritage and the experiences of individuals to shape learning. The interaction of these three sources of learning (genetic, cultural heritage, and experiences) is far from completely understood. It makes a difference, for example, whether the mind has been programmed by millions of years of hunter/gatherer experiences so that its flexibility to adjust in the very different modern world is limited, as is implied by the argument of evolutionary psychologists; or whether the mind has broader flexibility, as envisioned by the argument of Stephen J. Gould. If the evolutionary psychologists are correct then our modeling of the genetic-cultural mix is going to be weighted in favor of a better understanding of the nature of the special-purpose genetic features and their implications for our understanding of diverse cultures. Additionally, the success of human adjustment to the novel problems of a radically altered human environment is going to be more problematic. Clearly the universal "addiction" of humans to "non-rational" explanations as embodied in religions, superstitions, fundamentalist creeds, has as its source some innate properties of the mind that produce such beliefs. A better understanding of the forces making for such beliefs is a critical part of the agenda for a better understanding of the choices that direct societal change.[7]

It makes a difference whether the mind is innately logical and works like a computer, as envisioned by the classical cognitive scientists, or functions on the basis of pattern-based reasoning, as envisioned by connectionists. If the former is a correct understanding, then the work of AI researchers should bear rich fruit in improving our understanding of the process of reasoning and learning. Connectionists suggest a very different view in which pattern-based reasoning has different implications for approaching novel problems and for learning. If the learning process is pattern based rather than symbol based it suggests different abilities to confront and resolve novel problems.

The collective learning integral to Hayek's view of cultural evolution consisted of the intergenerational accumulation of knowledge, tools, attitudes, values, and institutions which had evolved by selective elimination of less suitable forms of conduct. They had met the slow test of time in an evolutionary process of trial and error. The culture of a society, in consequence of this evolution, embodied the distilled experience of the past, an experience that vastly exceeded the knowledge anyone could accumulate independently in a single lifetime. When we graft this point to Adam Smith's fundamental insight that the division of labor was not simply the way to make more effective use of our abilities but the major source of increasing our productivity, then the growth in the stock of knowledge embodied in a culture is intimately tied to increasing specialization and division of labor. But because the division of labor produces a division of knowledge and different kinds of knowl-

---

[7] Boyer (2001) is a good initial exploration.

edge are organized in different ways, the coordination of knowledge requires more than a set of prices to be effective in solving human problems. The implication is that the institutional structure will play a critical role in the degree to which diverse knowledge will be integrated and available to solve problems as economies become more complex. The knowledge problem, to cite Hayek, "is the problem of finding a method that not only best utilizes the knowledge dispersed among the individual members of society but also best uses their abilities of discovering and exploring new things" (Hayek 1979, 190).

This last point requires elaboration. As pointed out in chapter 2, uncertainty can be reduced by the accretion of knowledge. But what **kind** of knowledge? Knowledge that makes the individual more skilled at his/her specialty, or specialization and division of labor knowledge that increases his/her ability to deal with the wider world? Obviously there is a trade off between accuracy and variety. The more variety the agent possesses the better can he/she contend with an ever more complex environment that is a concomitant part of a world of specialization; but the more accuracy he/she possesses the more he/she can reduce uncertainty in that dimension of existence. Moreover, specialization introduces a specific kind of transaction cost—that of ascertaining the (measurement and performance) characteristics of goods and services acquired which are alien to one's specialized knowledge. In developed societies like the United States we "solve" this problem by an elaborate structure of institutions, organizations, and, broadly, the artifactual structure which provides warranties, guarantees, and the necessary informational structure to deal effectively with the vast range of goods and services available to us. There is, however, nothing automatic about the provision of such an artifactual structure.[8] Indeed successful development entails a complex structure of institutions and symbolic storage systems to integrate at low costs of transacting the dispersed knowledge of modern complex systems; and the failure to achieve such integration is at the heart of development problems.

It also is important to keep in mind that the foundations of the society are built on the beliefs of the players. Brian Loasby (1999) states the issues clearly as follows:

[8] For an elaboration of this argument, see Martens (1999).

The construction of economic models gives absolute priority to logical connections, both in the modeling process and in the conception of economic agents as rational actors. But logical operations determine only a small proportion of human actions; and even when they do, they depend on the knowledge base from which the premises are drawn, only a small proportion of which is logically ordered. Because our theories of evolutionary economics are appraised as the product of rigorous thought, there is a danger of exaggerating the role in economic progress of logical structures of conscious rationality at the expense of evolving capabilities, even in science-based industries. It is the growth of knowledge about how to get things done that has been the central phenomenon of economic evolution.

The development of "theoretic culture" as discussed in chapter 3 was the key to this economic evolution.

The institutional structure that has evolved determines who the strategic actors are and how they can effect their choices. The scaffolding discussed in chapter 5 gives us a brief summary of the issues. But an important corollary stems from the nature of that structure. The decision rules determined by the society will play the critical role in shaping whose choices matter and how they matter. The way humans structure the decision-making process determines whose beliefs matter. In terms of formal institutions this is the subject of political economy and although the literature is voluminous and immense progress has been made in our scholarly understanding of various aspects of the subject we still have little understanding of dynamic aspects.

A fundamental unknown is the way the informal constraints evolve. What is their relationship to changes in the formal rules? How do they evolve? How much is conscious, deliberate change and how much is incremental, non-deliberate in nature? And what is the contribution of changing informal constraints to overall cultural change? The growing literature on informal constraints is beginning to give us some answers to these questions.[9] Clearly the informal constraints are an integral part of the institutional framework that structures human interaction. Some may arise as a result of the uncoordinated actions of individuals. Conventions may be hit upon accidentally and then transmitted by imita-

---

[9] An excellent survey is contained in Ben-Ner and Putterman (1998).

tion. Many of them act to supplement, extend, or modify formal rules. Some, such as traditions of feuding, are clearly negative sum games and we are left with the puzzle of their persistence.

Our concern here is with the implications of informal constraints for economic performance and, particularly, the sources of their change. Informal constraints directly influence transaction costs. Norms of honesty, integrity, reliability lower transaction costs. The popularity of the term social capital (coined by the late James Coleman) reflects the recognition of the kinds of norms and values that facilitate exchange in various kinds of markets. Avner Greif has done the most systematic study (1994a and forthcoming a) of the effect of cultural values upon economic performance in comparing Genoese traders with traders who had adopted the cultural and social attributes of Islamic society in the Mediterranean trade of the eleventh and twelfth centuries. He detected systematic differences in their organizational structure traceable to contrasting individualist versus collectivist behavioral beliefs. The traders from the Islamic world developed in-group social communication networks to enforce collective action. While effective in relatively small homogeneous ethnic groups, such networks did not lend themselves to the impersonal exchange that arises with the growing size of markets and diverse ethnic traders. In contrast, the Genoese developed bilateral enforcement mechanisms which entailed the creation of formal legal and political organizations for monitoring and enforcing agreements— an institutional/organizational path that permitted and led to more complex trade and exchange.

What gives rise to or leads to changes in norms? Robert Putnam (1993), in an influential study contrasting performance in different parts of Italy, maintains that the contrasting social capital in North versus South Italy had its origins eight centuries earlier as a consequence of different patterns of hierarchically imposed controls versus voluntaristic sources of solving problems. The study by Platteau and Hayami cited in chapter 5 traces the development of norms to antecedent material and political structures. In the case of Africa, redistributive norms are alleged to have emerged in the context of low population density and abundant land. Because land commands little value in sub-Saharan Africa, private property rights on land have not become well established and therefore social stratification in rural communities based on land ownership has not evolved as it has in population-abundant, land-scarce Asia. "In such societies fairness rules that repress individuals who try to emancipate themselves economically are often rooted in a typically pre-rationalist magical worldview. In conditions of extreme vulnerability to the vagaries of nature, it is actually not surprising that belief systems incorporating supernatural agencies are believed to be ultimately responsible for the supply of food and other necessities. Effort applied by individuals and the production achieved are viewed as two separate things that are not causally related"(1998, 408). In such a context luck determines differential success and the benefit of such good fortune ought not to be confined to the prize winner. Also "there is fear that, if left free to choose, individuals with a high realized income will be tempted to evade their solidarity obligations and to defect altogether from mutual insurance mechanisms (since by accumulating their surplus income, they can self-insure effectively)." Redistributive norms in such a context can be viewed as taxation designed to curb "positional race for status." As discussed briefly in chapter 4, this view of the source of norms is controversial and at odds with the conclusion of the systematic study being undertaken in a variety of cultures by anthropologists; but it does resonate in terms of the general problem of the difficulty in making the transition from a belief system geared to solving problems of the physical environment to one confronting solutions to problems of the human environment.

Ultimately economic performance is a consequence of both the general economic rules that are in place and their enforcement characteristics (the property rights structure) and the specific institutional structure of each market—factor, product, or political. That is, the incentive structure for each market will differ from that of another market at a moment of time and also will change with its changing characteristics over time. Because there is a widespread prejudice among many neo-classical economists that simply an absence of government intervention is a sufficient condition for good economic performance in a particular market, it is important to stress that the performance characteristics of any market are a function of the set of constraints imposed by institutions (formal rules—including those by government—informal norms, and the enforcement characteristics) that determine the incentive structure in that market. As noted in the discussion of institutional change in chapter 5, if the incentives reward piracy then that will be the outcome. Any economist who doubts the importance of this observation has only to examine the characteristics of various factor and product markets in Russia in the 1990s to be convinced that it is the incentive structure derived from the institutional framework that is decisive. The rash of entrepreneurial malfeasance in large U.S. corporations in 2001–2 has reflected the evolution of an institutional framework that has altered relative prices to provide incentives for such anti-social behavior.

Moreover as technology, relative prices, and other external constraints change, so will the performance of the affected market change and there is no guarantee that institutions will automatically adjust to maintain the efficiency of the affected market. The crucial point is to recognize that efficient markets are created by structuring them to have low costs of transacting and these conditions will vary with each kind of market and with each market over time. Making the necessary changes over time leads us to the dilemma imposed by path dependence.

Path dependence is a fact of history and one of the most enduring and significant lessons to be derived from studying the past. The difficulty of fundamentally altering paths is evident and suggests that the learning process by which we arrive at today's institutions constrains future choices. It is more than simply that the organizations brought into existence by the existing institutional matrix owe their survival and well-being to that matrix and therefore will attempt to prevent changes that would adversely affect their well-being. It is also that the belief system underlying the institutional matrix will deter radical change. A major frontier of scholarly research is to do the empirical work necessary to identify the precise sources of path dependence so that we can be far more precise about its implications.

The long run economic success of western economies has induced a widespread belief that economic growth now is built into the system, in contrast to the experience of the previous ten millenia when growth was episodic and frequently non-existent. Since much of the world either still does not share in the growth experience or has only recently experienced growth, it is still an open question whether in fact that supposition is correct. It is important to understand that experiencing economic growth for fifteen or twenty years is not a guarantee that it is built into the system. Latin American economies have experienced stop-and-go growth for several centuries. Adaptive efficiency—the kind of efficiency that has characterized the United States and western Europe—entails a set of institutions that readily adapt to the shocks, disturbances, and ubiquitous uncertainty that characterize every society over time. The foundation of these flexible institutions resides in widely held beliefs embodied in the informal constraints of the society. While Part II discusses this issue, it is important to understand that we do not know how to create these conditions in a short period of time. In the Western world it has been an evolutionary product of centuries of institutional change.

V

We conclude this chapter by putting the issues raised in the foregoing pages in the context of the overall issues of this study: What do we mean by economic change, how is it related to the sources of institutional change described in chapter 5, and how much light have we shed on the *process* by the discussion in this chapter?

Economic change consists of a change in the material and physical well-being of humans broadly conceived to include change that can be quantified not only in national and personal income data, in physical measures of human well-being, but also in the less precisely measured but important aspects of human well-being embodied in non-market economic activity.

The growth in the stock of knowledge is the fundamental underlying determinant of the upper bound of human well-being. If that were the whole key our story would be a relatively simple one; but it is the complex interplay between the stock of knowledge, institutions, and demographic factors that shapes the process of economic change.

Institutional change is the structural change humans impose on human interaction with the intention of producing certain outcomes. To the extent that institutional change alters outcomes as intended by the actors responsible, there is an identity between intentions and outcomes (although there is no implication that the intention of the players is improved overall economic performance). A major part of this study, however, is concerned with the degree to which the beliefs of the players not only accurately reflect "reality" but also accurately forecast the behavior of the players to produce the intended outcome. An immense amount of economic change has been the unanticipated result of institutional change that reflected a significant gap between intentions and outcomes as a result of "faulty" beliefs. The fault may lie in not understanding the situation correctly but also in the revised institutional structure not altering behavior in intended ways.

Where the institutional framework is complemented by an elaborate artifactual structure and the institutional alterations are built on sound knowledge of their properties, outcomes are most likely to come close to intentions. With the development of external symbolic storage and the increasing informational richness of such systems, the mind has vastly increased its capacity to solve cognitive tasks. But at the same time humans have been developing increasingly complex environments that challenge those cognitive capacities.

The institutional framework constructed to produce political choices is a central source of outcomes diverging from intentions because as described in the preceding paragraphs, political markets reflect imperfect knowledge between principals and agents and are typically characterized by high costs of transacting. While an institutional structure will prevent cycling it is not clear what institutional structure will produce the desired welfare outcomes. But it is important to note that the key to improved performance is some combination of formal rules and informal constraints and the task we face is to achieve an understanding of exactly what combination will produce the desired results both at a moment of time and over time.

The fallibility of humans in attempting to structure their environment produces outcomes at odds with intentions, whether the intentions were improving economic performance or lining the pockets of the players. It is something else again exactly what the intentions of the players are. The overall direction of economic change will reflect the aggregate of choices made by political and economic entrepreneurs with widely diverse objectives, most of them not concerned with the consequences for overall performance. When economic markets are so structured that the players compete via price and quality rather than at

79

non-productive margins then the Smithian result ensues. But the outcome is a mixture of both economic and political decisions that in the aggregate affect the performance in individual political and economic markets as well as determine the direction of the economy as a whole. And at any moment of time the players are constrained by path dependence—the limits to choices arising from the combination of beliefs, institutions, and artifactual structure that have been inherited from the past.

PART II

THE ROAD AHEAD

Introduction

THE KEY to building a foundation to understand the process of economic change is beliefs—both those held by individuals and shared beliefs that form belief systems. The explanation is straightforward; the world we have constructed and are trying to understand is a construction of the human mind. It has no independent existence outside the human mind; thus our understanding is unlike that in the physical sciences, which can employ reductionism to understand, and expand comprehension of, the physical world. Physical scientists, when they seek a greater understanding of some puzzle in the physical world, can build from the fundamental unit of their science to explore the dimension of the problem they seek to comprehend. The social sciences do not have anything comparable to genes, protons, neutrons, elements to build upon. The whole structure that makes up the foundation of human interaction is a construct of the human mind and has evolved over time in an incremental process; the culture of a society is the cumulative aggregate of the surviving beliefs and institutions.

It is important to understand that while the constructs humans create are a subjective function of the human mind, humans are continually testing the constructs (read theories) against evidence to see if they have explanatory value. But note that both evidence and theories are constructs and both at best are very imperfect mirrors of what we are trying to comprehend and therefore control.

It is essential to remember that the constructs humans create are a blend of "rational" beliefs and "non-rational" ones (superstitions, religions, myths, prejudices) that together shape the choices that are made. Our task is to understand the way belief systems evolve and the complicated social structures that have evolved as a consequence; more than that, we attempt an understanding of the way the structure is evolving over time.

Therefore we must explore the way consciousness interacts with diverse experiences that produce diverse cultural—institutional—patterns. We must account for the origins of belief systems that either

83

provide a favorable milieu for the creation of productive political and economic institutions or conversely thwart the creation of such institutions. Whether the institutional constructs create a favorable or an unfavorable milieu for improving economic performance, we have to understand the complex structure that has evolved.

The new institutional economics, focusing as it does on the incentive structure humans construct, should provide a much deeper understanding than we currently possess of the complex interlinks involved in the interdependent economic, political, and social world we have constructed. Formal (neo-classical) economic theory ignores this structure and therefore is of limited value for coming to grips with these issues. Information networks developed by sociologists explore the complex interlinks essential to undertaking all kinds of economic activity.[1] The complex information channels developed in the Silicon Valley to realize the potential of the computer revolution go far beyond the formal structure of firms and markets developed in standard economics. Transaction cost economics provides us with an opening to widen and deepen economic analysis to confront these issues. But very little work has been done to understand the complex interdependence of the evolving social structure the human mind has created. Without that understanding we are basically crippled in attempting to improve the economic performance of societies. There are four fundamental stumbling blocks which were implicit in Adam Smith's *Wealth of Nations* but have been ignored by modern neo-classical economists because they involve explicit institutional analysis.

1. There is the movement from personal to impersonal exchange. Such a move has posed, and still does pose, a fundamental obstacle to realizing the potential envisioned by Adam Smith when he viewed the wealth of nations as being a function of the size of markets. The necessary institutional changes required to realize the gains from large-scale (and impersonal) markets require fundamental rethinking at odds with our genetic heritage.

2. Adam Smith's specialization and division of labor—the necessary condition for achieving such markets—is really specialization of knowledge.

---

[1] For a particularly interesting illustration of the complex interrelationships involved in genetic research see Powell (1996).

The problem of integrating this dispersed knowledge at low costs of trans-acting is one that is not completely solved by a price system. It requires novel institutional and organizational connections to overcome the public goods attributes, externalities, and information asymmetries that prevent the price system from fully integrating distributed knowledge.

3. All well-functioning factor and product markets must be structured to provide incentives for the players to compete at those margins, and those margins alone, that induce growing productivity. Only then do we realize Smith's beneficent result. Moreover, in a dynamic world with changing tech-nology, information costs, and politics there is nothing automatic about the structure changing in response to these changing parameters to continue to produce efficient markets.

4. Well-functioning markets require government, but not just any gov-ernment will do. There must be institutions that limit the government from preying on the market. Solving the development problem therefore requires the crafting of political institutions that provide the necessary underpin-nings of public goods essential for a well-functioning economy and at the same time limit the discretion and authority of government and of the individual actors within government.

The chapters that follow outline the general contours of the evolving human environment, explore the institutional intricacies of successful and unsuccessful economic development and the process of change in the historical experience of diverse economies, and then derive implica-tions for understanding economic change and for improving economic performance. More than anything else, what follows is an agenda for research; I hope that it will provide the stimulus for pursuing that agenda.

The Evolving Human Environment

A NECESSARY PRECONDITION to understanding the evolving human environment is understanding the revolutionary changes resulting in the "conquest" of the physical environment: those changes provide the context for the evolving human environment. The conquest of the physical environment has been a result of the growth of knowledge about the physical world and its application to solving problems of economic scarcity and human well-being. I have described, in an earlier study (North 1981), the first and second economic revolutions. The first economic revolution was the development of agriculture beginning in the eighth millennium B.C. The second was the application of scientific knowledge (with its origins in the Renaissance) to solving economic and demographic problems, the result of which was an immense leap in economic productivity and human well-being and longevity. I will outline the conquest of the physical environment and then describe, as best we understand it, the evolving features of the human environment and explore the challenges involved in understanding it.

I

The background to the conquest of the physical environment has been a complex interplay between initial alterations in the physical characteristics of humanoids and cultural changes. We begin by noting that humans were differentiated from other primates some four million years ago; they remained hunters and gatherers up to the Neolithic revolution. The genetic imprint from these four million years provides a deep common denominator to mental processes. The increase in the size of the human brain, an erect stature, and the development of vocal chords enormously accelerated the cultural complexity that came about with more sophisticated tools but particularly with language. The result was

87

the development of different languages and patterns of organization, and the adoption of agriculture in societies. As we move up in time the complexity of human activity and interaction increases. The development of city states, increasing specialization and division of labor, and the beginning of dynastic rule in Egypt would be followed by the variety of civilizations that emerged in China, the Indus valley, Mesopotamia, and othe regions. We have a bewildering array of different polities, economies, and societies even before getting to the last two millennia.[1]

The hospitality of the environment to human development has played a critical role in the differential patterns of development. Not only has climate been important but the interaction between animals and humans, the consequent patterns of immune system developments, and the devastating consequences of exposure to pathogens that were not a part of the original environment have all played a major part in the distribution of human activity.[2] It is only as we approach modern times with the systematic application of scientific knowledge to problems of economic scarcity, the conquest of many infectious diseases, and the development of air conditioning that the physical environment ceases to play such a critical role. But even today malaria and the tsetse fly exert a major influence on human settlement.

The last two thousand years have been characterized by unprecedented change. This change has been facilitated by the development of external memory sources which have, through the development of increasingly complex symbolic storage systems, permitted the rise of complex societies. From the development of writing to the modern computer is a lengthy story of increasing ability of humans to deal with the ever increasing complexity of the human environment.[3] The rather myopic vision of western scholars has not only been geographically focused on the rise of the Western world to the neglect of the rest of

[1] See North (1981) for an ambitious, if brief, survey of human economic history since the Neolithic revolution.

[2] Diamond (1997) is an account of the complex interrelationship of humans and animals and the consequent implications for human development or non-development. Valuable as this book is for pointing us to an understanding of the implications of different environments for early development, the analysis of later developments is devoid of an appreciation of the complexity of the institutional environment for development.

[3] For a fascinating account of this evolution see Donald (1991).

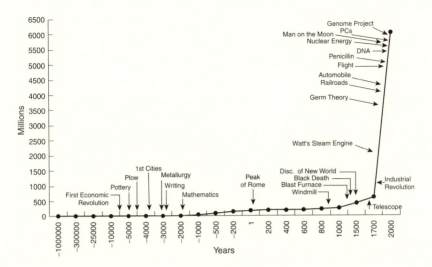

FIGURE 7.1. World Population, 1,000,000 B.C. Present. Source: Kremer (1990, 683); also adapted from Fogel (2003).

the world; it also has been temporally focused on the Industrial Revolution as the great watershed of economic—and indeed social—history to the neglect of the earlier centuries and also to the neglect of the social, political, and broadly institutional factors that underlie modern economic growth. The overall landscape must equally include the rise of the Western world and the "arrested" development of other civilizations, the acceleration of innovation in England and the long period of gradual change that preceded it.

Statistical data, to the extent that they exist, can get us part way in describing the magnitude of the changes in the landscape. They provide dramatic evidence of the revolutionary change in the human condition.

Man's subjugation of the uncertainties related to the physical environment is most clearly manifested in the explosive increases in population since the beginning of the modern age in the eighteenth century. Figure 7.1 illustrates this dramatic change along with major developments in knowledge, technological progress, and scientific breakthroughs that contributed to this explosive development. The consequence has been the immense jump in life expectancy (figure 7.2) and decline in infant mortality (figure 7.3). The consequent growing disparity between the developed and the less developed world, which has not

89

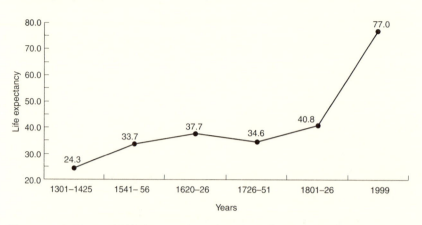

FIGURE 7.2. Years of Life Expectation at Birth in the United Kingdom, 1300–Present. Source: Maddison (2001, 29).

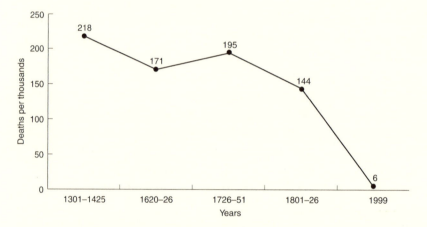

FIGURE 7.3. Deaths per Thousand in First Year of Life in the United Kingdom, 1300–1999. Maddison (2001, 29).

been able to take advantage of the application of science and technology to solving the problem of scarcity, is shown in table 7.1. In a world in which the uncertainties were associated with the physical environment most people lived in the countryside. The development of the interdependent world that characterizes the complex structure of the human environment is reflected in the growing number of large cities, particularly since 1900 (figure 7.4) and the growing percentage of population living in cities with more than five thousand inhabitants (figure 7.5). That transformation from rural to urban has reflected a basic alteration

TABLE 7.1.
Per Capita GDP, Developed and Undeveloped World, 1000–1998

	(1990 international dollars)					
	1000	1500	1600	1700	1820	1998
Average Developed	405	704	805	907	1,130	21,470
Average Undeveloped	440	535	548	551	573	3,102
Ratio, Developed to Undeveloped	0.92	1.32	1.47	1.65	1.97	6.92

Source: Maddison (2001, 46).

in output from agricultural and other extractive activities to manufacturing and eventually to services. It is not that extractive activities have been absolutely declining—the United States is a world-leading exporter of agricultural goods; rather it is that productivity increase has permitted ever expanding output in agriculture and manufacturing output with relatively less input of productive factors, at the same time that an ever growing demand for services has resulted in an ever greater percentage of resources going into services. Some of the services, such as medicine, are income elastic (as we get richer we devote an increasing percentage of income to them) but the major reason for the growth of services is that resources are devoted to transacting. Transaction costs are the costs involved in exchange; and as specialization and division of labor have increased, so has the number of exchanges, each of which has entailed devoting resources to that exchange. Banking, insurance, finance, wholesale and retail trade, as well as a good part of government activity are all part of the transaction sector. And then inside the firm there are ever increasing numbers of accountants, lawyers, and others devoted to facilitating exchange in the complex economic world of impersonal exchange. The movement from personal to impersonal exchange always increases total transaction costs but the consequence is a drastic reduction in production costs, which more than offset the increased resources going into transacting—and was responsible for the dramatic growth of modern economies. Figure 7.6 charts the overall growth of the transaction sector in the American economy from 1870 to 1970 (with extrapolation to 2000). This growth has largely reflected the growing specialization and division of labor and consequent imper-

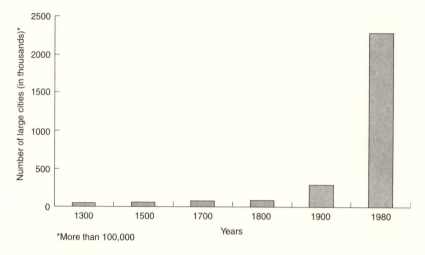

FIGURE 7.4. Number of Large Cities in the World (1300–1980). Source: Bairoch (1988, 502).

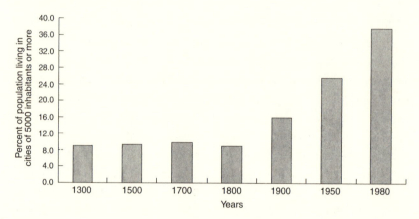

FIGURE 7.5. Urbanization in the World. Source: Bairoch (1988, 495).

sonal exchange although we should note that some of it has reflected transaction cost increases because of restrictions on productivity growth via restrictions on competition and monopoly.

Ever increasing international interdependence is reflected in the growth of international trade. Even though domestic growth was a dramatic feature of the new human environment, the increasing interdependence of the modern world is dramatically illustrated by the growth of exports as a percentage of GNP in figure 7.7.

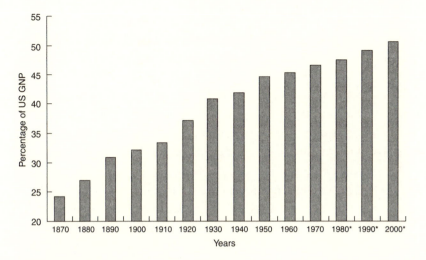

FIGURE 7.6. Transaction Costs as a Percentage of U.S. GNP, 1870–2000. Source: Wallis and North (1988).

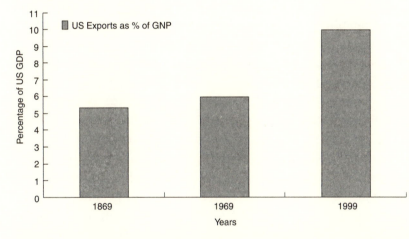

FIGURE 7.7. International Trade, 1869–1999. Source: Author's calculations from U.S. Department of Commerce (1976) and U.S. Department of the Treasury (2001).

The conquest of the physical environment has reduced or eliminated the traditional sources of human uncertainty but the evolving human environment has replaced them with new and more deadly challenges to human well-being and even human survival. The revolutionary technological changes that have made possible a world of material plenty

93

have also been the source of weapons of such destructive power that they can destroy cities, countries, and indeed all human life. The twentieth century was witness to more casualties than had occurred in all previous history (figure 7.8).

Throughout most of history there were relatively homogeneous standards of living across countries; the gap between developed and undeveloped is a striking feature of the past century. The inability of the third world to exploit the promise of modern technology is in startling contrast to the developed world and reflects an institutional framework and underlying beliefs that prevent the development of impersonal exchange and the consequent productivity developments (figure 7.9).[4]

Over time it is the variety of responses of humans to different environments expressed in terms of languages, customs, technologies, and organization that stands out. The differential hospitality of the physical environment to human development explains much of the historical difference in human well-being. But increasingly, as scientific knowledge has modified the differences in the physical environment, the complex interplay between demography, the stock of knowledge, and the institutions of societies shapes performance (although the long shadow of the past plays an important part in influencing the present).

New research by demographers has begun to give us an understanding of and explanation for both the size of population over time and also the quality of population—both the physical quality and the "human capital" quality. Substantial progress has been made in our understanding of changing sources of fertility and mortality, of nutritional status, of morbidity, and of those aspects of population quality broadly encompassed in the literature sometimes characterized as the new economics of the household. It is in demographic change that we are witness to the most dramatic consequences of the conquest of the physical environment.

[4] The foregoing tables and charts summarize the enormous changes associated with the development of the human environment but a word of caution is necessary. The data are surrogates for complex, multidimensional aspects of human well-being, and as a vast literature on income accounting attests, are rather poor surrogates. The measurement problems are even greater when exploring these dimensions over time. An old but still useful account is that contained in Adelman and Morris (1971).

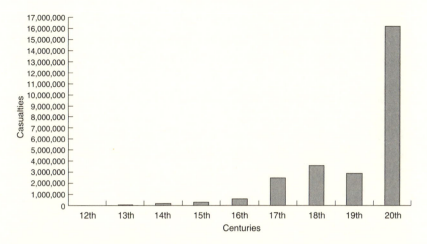

FIGURE 7.8. Casualties in England, France, Russia, and Austria-Hungary, Twelfth–Twentieth Centuries. Source: Peace Pledge Union, <www.ppu.org.uk/war/facts/nine_century.html>.

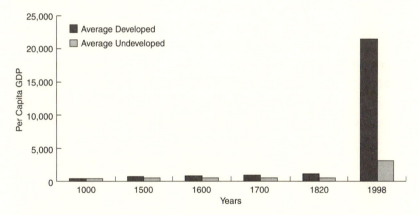

FIGURE 7.9. Per Capita GDP in the Developed and Undeveloped World, 1000–1998. Source: Maddison (2001).

Pioneering work by Robert Fogel and his associates has detailed the extraordinary changes in human demography. Specifically "during the last 300 years, particularly during the last century, humans have gained an unprecedented degree of control over their environment—a degree of control so great that it sets them apart not only from all other species, but also from all previous generations of Homo Sapiens. This new degree of control has enabled Homo Sapiens to increase its

95

average body size by over 50%, to increase its average longevity by more than 100%, and to improve greatly the robustness and capacity of vital organ systems" (Fogel and Costa 1997). Fogel's initial concentration was on nutritional status and derived inspiration from Thomas McKeown's influential study *The Modern Rise of Population* (1976) which argued that medical advances cannot explain the observed mortality decline. More recent research that Fogel and others have done recognizes that nutritional status is affected not only by nutritional intake but also by disease and it is the conquest of infectious diseases that has been critical.

The research of Fogel and others shows us that time has seen a pronounced increase in the quality, as well as quantity of human beings. The Human Development Index (HDI) of the United Nations Development Program (UNDP) is one attempt to measure quality of human beings. It is simply the sum of normalized indices of per capita national income, life expectancy at birth, and the adult literacy rate. Costa and Steckel (1995) estimate HDIs for the United States, 1800–1970 (figure 7.10). Another striking aspect of the improvement in the quality is the lower incidence of chronic disease. As Fogel (2003) shows, we not only are living longer—we are living more healthily (figure 7.11). Major breakthroughs were new methods of preventing transmission of disease starting in the mid-nineteenth century; new vaccines to prevent certain diseases starting in the 1890s; and new drugs to cure infectious diseases starting in the late 1930s. Obviously, new knowledge was the key to this revolutionary demographic change; but what role was played by institutions? Richard Easterlin (1999) argues convincingly that the institutional developments that underlie this revolution were not those of the market (which underpinned the increase in economic well-being) but new institutions centering on the public health system. "The functions of this system have included in varying degrees health education, regulation, compulsion, and the financing or direct provision of services. The establishment of a public health system has required acceptance of social responsibility for the control of major infectious disease. This shift in norms came about as the advance of biomedical knowledge increasingly pointed to factors beyond individual control as the primary source of disease."

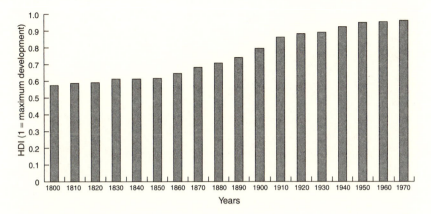

FIGURE 7.10. Costa and Steckel Estimates of Human Development Index, 1800–1970. Source: Costa and Steckel (1995).

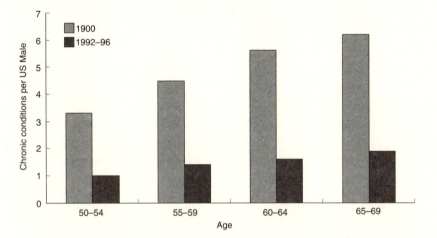

FIGURE 7.11. Age and Number of Chronic Conditions per U.S. Male in 1900 and the 1990s. Source: Fogel (2003, table 4.5).

Recent research has increased our understanding of the changing stock of knowledge although that research has primarily focused on just one aspect—but a major one—of that change, namely the sources underlying changes in technological knowledge. While increasing human command over nature has been an integral part of our history, this technological development has accelerated as societies have become more complex and then been revolutionized in the past several centuries by the development and application of science to technology.

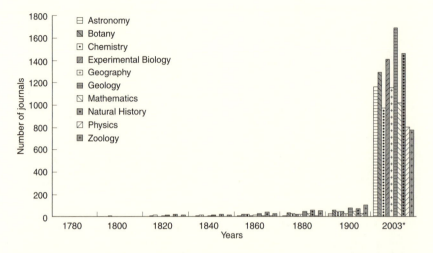

FIGURE 7.12. Scientific Periodicals, 1780–Present. Source: Law and Kim (2003).

* Taken from the HOLLIS Catalog of Harvard University. Number of titles in HOL-LIS Catalog equals the number of records returned from subject keyword searches of the HOLLIS Journal's database.

The development of science in the sixteenth and seventeenth centuries and its application to solving problems of scarcity beginning, for the most part, in the late nineteenth century in the German chemical industry is a well worked story. Joel Mokyr (2000) paints a more complicated story than the usual one of economic historians. An intricate mixture of new knowledge, applied knowledge, and techniques were integrated together by institutions and organizations to realize the potential of this knowledge. In recent work Mokyr (2002) has stressed the development of the institutional framework that has undergirded this development.

The specialization and division of labor that has been a key feature of growth has as an essential feature specialization in knowledge, which has resulted in immense increase in human productivity. One indicator of this specialization in knowledge is the extraordinary growth of specialized scientific journals in the twentieth century (see figure 7.12). The integration of this specialized knowledge with low costs of transacting requires more than an effective price system. Institutions and organizations were necessary to supplement the price system where externalities, information asymmetries, and free rider problems had to be overcome. The increasingly dispersed knowledge of modern societies requires a complex structure of institutions and organizations to integrate and apply that knowledge. The implication is fundamental to this study: The growth of knowledge is dependent on complementary institutions which will facilitate and encourage such growth and there is nothing automatic about such development.

The foregoing discussion has been focused narrowly on knowledge directly relevant to the performance of economies; but as emphasized in early chapters, we must equally be concerned with knowledge in its wider context. We know much less about the overall growth of the stock of knowledge and about the way evolving perceptions and beliefs have influenced the direction of that growth. A thorny question is just what we mean by knowledge since human decision making has, throughout history, been guided by possessed beliefs that have more often than not proven to be incorrect. Indeed the heart of this study is about the uncertainty humans face and the way they have dealt with that uncertainty. Are beliefs knowledge? Medical beliefs in the early nineteenth century were as often counter-productive as productive, "centering, as they did, on treatment by means of emetics, cathartics, diuretics, and bleeding" (Rosenberg 1979, 13). And such erroneous beliefs are not just a historical problem; a survey in Bangladesh in 1986 found that less than 30 percent of mothers believed that contaminated food or water might be responsible for diarrhea (Easterlin 1996, 15).

II

I want now to put together an outline of the evolving human landscape drawn from a combination of the material in Part I and the discussion of the transformation from the institutions geared to the physical environment to those built to deal with the human environment. The conclusions are strongly supported with the results of experimental studies both in the laboratory and in field studies.[5] The innate mental capacities of humans underlie personal exchange. These genetic features provide

---

[5] There is a rich trove of experimental research currently being undertaken to give us a better understanding of human behavior. In addition to the studies cited in earlier chapters Greif (forthcoming a) summarizes much of the ongoing work. An up-to-date summary can be found in Kevin McCabe (2003).

the framework for exchange and are the foundation of the structure of human interaction that characterizes societies throughout history. The recognition of decision-making roles and rights has allowed personal exchange to extend over wider areas.

An argument advanced in Part I was that beliefs reflected the diverse experiences that humans in different social and physical settings encountered. The diverse experiences produced different degrees of flexibility with respect to shifting from beliefs confronting the uncertainties associated with the physical environment to those capable of dealing with the complexities of the evolving human environment. In particular the successful transition of the Western world to dealing with these complexities as reflected in the development of impersonal exchange, integrating the specialized knowledge essential to effectively utilizing it in complex economic structures, and more or less successfully evolving the polities that undergirded these changes is in stark contrast to the less developed world whose poor economic performance has reflected inability to make the transition. Thus "traditional rural communities have characteristics that were well suited to meet past challenges. For example, sharing norms had more advantages than shortcomings when they were critically needed to preserving risk-pooling arrangements and maintain the long-term social cohesion of the community in a world pervaded by serious risks that could not be hedged otherwise" (Abraham and Platteau 2002, 25).

These are the characteristics of societies confronted by the uncertainties of the physical environment. The increasing opportunities provided as the environment changes to one in which the human environment poses the crucial issues entails a transformation in social organization of fundamental dimensions. "What is required is a shift from a status-based and coercive society that relies on mutual control, respect of ranks, and strictly enforced codes of generosity, to an open society where free entry and exit, democratic governance (including acceptance of dissent), competence criteria, and socio-economic differentiation are used as guiding principles or expressly allowed to operate" (ibid., 26).

The contrast between the institutions and beliefs geared to confronting the uncertainties of the physical environment and those constructed to confront the human environment is the key to understanding the process of change. Recent research in experimental economics is beginning to give us an understanding of the essential issues. The collectivist cultural beliefs that characterized the former environment produced an institutional structure geared to personal exchange whose cohesion and structure were built around strong personal ties. In contrast the individualistic framework that evolved in response to the new human environment relied less on personal ties and more on a formal structure of rules and enforcement mechanisms. Each structure fostered its own set of beliefs which shaped the evolving structure of the resultant polities, economies, and societies. With this background I want to describe three aspects of economic change which focus on the crucial characteristics of the changing human condition and will serve as an introduction to the following chapters.

1. Modern economic growth had as its source the growth in the stock of knowledge that is associated with the scientific revolution of the sixteenth and seventeenth centuries. What is the source of the attitudes, procedures, and experimental methods that characterized this revolution? It was a western phenomenon and obviously related to the institutional developments that led to the rise of the Western world from a relatively backward part of the world in the tenth century to its worldwide preeminence by the eighteenth century. But that story is a complicated one in which the direction of institutional change was influenced by many factors including the reciprocal interactions among the three strands of our analysis (demographic changes, the stock of knowledge, and institutions). And the institutional developments—political, economic, and social—in turn reflected the development of a belief system. Where did the belief system come from? I have argued elsewhere (North 1995b) that its origins are in the way religious beliefs (and reaction to those beliefs) evolved in medieval–early modern Europe and the way those beliefs in turn were heavily influenced by the unique experiences that characterized that part of the world.

2. The contrasting performance characteristics of economies geared to dealing with the physical environment and those constructed to deal with the human environment raise fundamental questions about the basic divergent patterns that have evolved to result in economic growth on the one hand and stagnation on the other. The issue is obviously one of the dynamics of change in which the ongoing experiences of a society gradually modify existing beliefs and hence the institutional

framework; the result may be adaptively efficient institutions that respond effectively to changes in the human environment or stagnation and increasingly dysfunctional attitudes and policies. Can we trace out the sequential patterns that produced these contrasting patterns?

3. Understanding modern economic growth entails setting the foregoing analysis into a broader context. There is a complex interplay among improving nutrition to permit humans to be more productive, the growth in the stock of useful knowledge applied to solve problems of human scarcity, political institutions (both formal and informal) directing humans to engage in productive activity, economic institutions that structure factor and product markets both at a moment of time and over time to be efficient, the growth in the size of the market to realize scale economies, educational investment to improve human capital—all of these contributed to modern economic growth. But there are also non-rational beliefs, technologies that give rise to weapons ever more powerful in destruction, the persistent intolerance of divergent beliefs, and the consequent continuous pattern of human self-destruction. How much of economic growth was a result of shrewd judgment in contrast to just plain good luck?

The Sources of Order and Disorder

ECONOMISTS seldom put the problem of order and disorder at the center of inquiry.[1] Historical—and contemporary—experience suggests that they should. Establishing and maintaining social order in the context of dynamic change has been an age-old dilemma of societies and continues to be a central problem in the modern world. Economic change produces changes in the absolute and relative income, economic status, and security of individuals and groups in a society and therefore is a breeding ground for disorder. Disorder (via revolution, for example) is endemic to all societies at some time; but while some societies quickly reestablish stable order, in others disorder persists for long periods of time and even when order is reestablished its survival is extremely fragile. The persistence of disorder is, on the face of it, puzzling because disorder increases uncertainty and typically the great majority of players are losers. It is not so puzzling when perceived in the context of human consciousness. Beliefs, both positive and normative, are at the heart of consciousness. We have not only a vision of the way an economy and society is working but a normative view of how it should be working and views about how it could be restructured to work better. Thus consciousness can lead to the construction of a set of beliefs that induce players to believe that revolution is a preferred alternative to a continuation of what is perceived as a deteriorating condition. At the other extreme, consciousness can lead to the construction of a set of beliefs in the "legitimacy" of a society. We need to explore under what conditions beliefs get activated to produce order and disorder.

[1] This chapter is largely derived from an essay by North, Summerhill, and Weingast (2000).

I

Order is a necessary (but not sufficient) condition for long-run economic growth. It is equally a necessary (but not sufficient) condition for the establishment and maintenance of the variety of conditions underlying freedom of person and property that we associate with a consensual or democratic society. Improving our understanding of the fundamental sources of order and disorder as well as the transition from one to the other is necessary for understanding economic change.

Order can be established and maintained via an authoritarian rule without the consent of the governed or it can be established and maintained via consent of the governed. The ideal type of each can be described as follows.

Authoritarian political order ideally exists when the participants find it in their interest, given their expectations about the actions of others, to obey the written or unwritten rules specified by the ruler. Conformity is usually attributed to some mixture of coercive force by the ruler and social norms such that individuals find it in their interest to behave in ways conducive to the existing social order. A common belief system which embodies social norms consistent with the policies of the ruler will reduce the use of coercion; and conversely, diverse belief systems or a common belief system at odds with the policies of the ruler will increase the ruler's reliance on coercion.

Consensual political order exists ideally when the participants find it in their interest, given their expectations about the actions of others, to obey the written or unwritten rules that call for respect for one another. Conformity is usually attributed to the internalization of social norms so that individuals want to behave in ways conducive to the existing social order and/or social control, which is exercised over potential social deviance by others. Shared mental models reflecting a common belief system will translate into a set of institutions broadly conceived to be legitimate.[2] Consensual political order requires that, in equilibrium, all members of society have an incentive to obey and enforce the rules and that a sufficient number are motivated to punish

---

[2] See Denzau and North (1994) for an elaboration of the cognitive science foundations of this argument.

potential deviants. The rules are binding providing, first, that the same people play the same game with the same pay-offs and risks; and second, that the uncertainties about the future remain constant.[3]

Both systems of order ideally have the following characteristics:

1. an institutional matrix that produces a set of organizations and establishes a set of rights and privileges;

2. a stable structure of exchange relationships in both political and economic markets;

3. an underlying structure that credibly commits the state to a set of political rules and enforcement that protects organizations and exchange relationships;

4. conformity as a result of some mixture of norm internalization and coercive enforcement.

The two types are at opposite ends of the spectrum of political organization and are seldom, if ever, realized in their pure form. Authoritarian rule can, and does, vary, from Josef Stalin terrorism to the "Singapore" model; and consensual order can vary from the direct democracy of some Swiss Cantons to the de facto single party rule that has characterized Mexican political order over the past decades. The important point that this comparison stresses is that order reduces uncertainty and therefore has some common characteristics that are considered a "good" in themselves and individuals and groups in society have frequently knowingly accepted authoritarian order in preference to disorder. A second point is that authoritarian and consensual rule tend to blend into each other in the middle of this spectrum where some mixture of coercion and social norms is the basis of order. Coercion is an essential part of consensual political order where decisions affecting the members of a society are made by less than unanimity of the members. Thus coercion and force are an integral part of both societies; the difference is the extent to which decision makers are influenced by the formal and particularly the informal constraints in the system.

Disorder increases uncertainty because rights and privileges of individuals and organizations are up for grabs, implying disruption of ex-

---

[3] See Calvert (1998) for a game theoretic modeling of the issues which illumines a number of critical issues in the establishment and maintenance of order.

isting exchange relationships in both political and economic markets; and conformity disappears as a result of disintegration of norms and/ or change in enforcement. Here we will look at the origins of disorder in economic change and then explore the stability conditions for the maintainence of order with economic change. We will do so by contrasting histories of United States and Latin American economies, which illustrate disorder and then recovery to stable order and revolution followed by prolonged disorder.

II

Disorder can result from changes which lead to a reduction of coercive enforcement of rules or from the weakening of norms of cooperation, which induces organizations to attempt radical changes in the rules of the game. One kind of change is an event that dislodges the old mechanisms that provided credible commitment in society without providing adequate substitutes. Examples of such events include the demise of a (authoritarian) ruler, but often they reflect a crisis that allows a sudden turnover in political power by groups who seek major political change. Crises may dislodge the old order in any of several ways. For example, an economic crisis limiting the resources that can be distributed may persuade some erstwhile supporters of the regime to oppose it, thereby destroying the consensus supporting the regime.

Another kind of change can arise from a set of incremental changes that persuade some individuals and groups that revolution is a lesser risk than a continuation of the incremental changes which are perceived to threaten the survival of one group. De Figuerido and Weingast (1999) summarize the steps in this process as follows:

1. A set of political entrepreneurs articulate a new set of beliefs in fundamental conflict with the existing order—beliefs that are held, at first, only by a small minority.

2. The opponents of these entrepreneurs act in ways that make these beliefs appear to be true, thus confirming the revolutionary beliefs in the eyes of the pivotal players. Thus events beyond the direct control of the new ideas proponents occur that lend some credence to these beliefs.

3. The result is a spread of the beliefs to some of the pivotal decision makers. When the pivotal decision makers accept the radically new beliefs, they provide sufficient political support for radical action.

III

The maintenance of order over long periods of time and the rapid reestablishment of order when a society undertakes radical change have distinguished societies like the United States from most of those in world history. The key is the establishment of institutions of impersonal exchange that constrain the players and limit political rule making. Over the past three-and-a-half centuries the United States (as it now is) has maintained a system of order with economic change including rapid recovery from a revolution gaining independence from England and from one of the most devastating civil wars in history. Moreover the economic growth that has occurred over this period has radically altered the incomes and status of groups in the society. In societies that have adaptive efficiency (North 1990b), the flexibility of the institutional matrix adjusts to resolve problems associated with fundamental economic change. Four propositions for the maintenance of political order in the face of economic change can give us some insight into adaptive efficiency.

The first proposition concerns the relationship of a shared belief system about the legitimate ends of government and the rights of citizens. All rights accorded to citizens—whether personal, economic, religious, civil, or political—imply limits to the behavior of political officials. The key to political order is the establishment of credible bounds on the behavior of political officials. Citizen rights and the implied bounds of government must be self-enforcing for political officials in that transgressing them would jeopardize a political leader's future. The creation of a shared belief system in a society reflects the development (usually over a long period of time) of social norms with respect to the legitimate limits of behavior of political officials.

The second proposition holds that successful constitutions limit the stakes of politics in part by assigning citizen rights and placing other limits on government decision making. The third proposition states

107

that property and personal rights must be well defined so that it is evident to citizens when these rights are being transgressed. The fourth holds that the state must provide credible commitments to respect these rights, thus providing protection against opportunism and expropriation by public officials.

Underlying these propositions is an institutional matrix that not only specifies these conditions in the formal rules but, equally important, is undergirded by strongly held social norms that imbed these values into the culture of the society. Because this cultural conditioning of a society usually takes place over generations it is fundamentally difficult to establish stable consensual order in societies that have experienced persistent disorder. In such cases authoritarian order may very well be preferred by the members of that society.

IV

American political, social, and economic history has been characterized by relative stability in the colonial era up to the end of the Seven Years War; instability and then revolution until 1781; the reestablishment of order and rapid economic development to be interrupted again by the Civil War between 1861 and 1865; and then the relatively rapid reestablishment of order and revival of economic growth that persisted thereafter. The main contours of this story can be outlined in terms of the analytical framework advanced in the previous section.[4]

The British Empire of the eighteenth century had multiple levels of government, each with its relatively well defined sphere of authority. Until the end of the Seven Years War in 1763, the British role in North America was limited to empire-wide public goods, notably security and international trade. Colonial assemblies, working with the British governor, held broad authority over local public goods, property rights, religious freedom, and contract enforcement, subject to some constraints of British law. The institutions of the empire placed considerable constraints on the British role within the individual American col-

---

[4] This account is drawn from North et al. (2000). A longer and more detailed account can be found in Rakove et al. (2001).

onies. British institutions created a common market within the empire, preventing individual colonies from raising trade barriers.

The pervasive French threat bound together both sides of the Atlantic in a relationship based on common interests. Because both sides needed each other, they were able to create and adhere to a system of political and economic autonomy inherent in the empire's federal structure. Although each side might be tempted to cheat, both sides found the empire's federal structure convenient. Indeed the strict line between the system-wide issues of trade and security and all other domestic issues within the colonies (such as religious freedom, taxation, property, and social regulation) created a credible commitment mechanism. In this system, deviations by either side were easy to detect. In terms of the four propositions for consensual political order, the empire's federal structure created a natural focal solution, making actions easy to police by either side.

Over the one hundred years prior to 1763, the British came to accept local political freedom in exchange for the colonist's acceptance of British control over the empire, including trading restrictions on the colonists. The institutions of the empire combined with the shared belief system supporting these institutions together underpinned cooperation from both sides of the Atlantic. Various changes in British policy toward the empire after 1763 threatened this system. Two were critical. First, although the war removed the French threat, it did so at a huge financial price, leaving Britain with the largest debt ever. The British turned to the colonies to finance a portion of the debt. Second, the French defeat greatly changed the empire. Prior to the defeat, the American colonies represented a major portion of the empire. Anything that hurt the American colonies hurt the empire. After the Seven Years War, this was not necessarily true. In the new and much larger empire, the British might reasonably design empire-wide policies to govern the system that might harm one part. Additionally, the colonies had much less need for the British security umbrella and thus less reason to conform to British interests.

These changes led many Americans to conclude that Britain would no longer observe the principles of federalism within the empire. This view was especially strong among an emerging radical group. This group argued that the precedent of the British directly intervening in colonial affairs through taxes meant the end of liberty, including the end of autonomy for colonial assemblies, and hence all that the colonies held dear. With this precedent established, the group went on to say, the British could alter other policies at their discretion. In the beginning most Americans paid little attention to the radicals, whose noise about liberty seemed not to ring true. The British had yet to provide much cause for believing that they intended major policy changes. Further, moderates and opponents both feared that the alternative to British rule was worse. But a succession of policies of the British, from the request that the colonies provide for the quartering of British troops in 1766 to the Tea Act of 1773, induced strong reactions in the Colonies and provided striking evidence to support the radicals. As the radicals suggested from the beginning, the new British policies threatened American liberty.

In short the sudden emergence of disorder in America reflected the principles articulated above. The defeat of the French helped dislodge the old system, leading to changes in British behavior and policy within the Empire. In reaction, American radicals articulated a new idea, one at first on the fringe of American beliefs, namely that the British actions represented the end of liberty. Early in the controversy with Britain, the politically pivotal moderates disagreed with the radicals. Yet British actions provided evidence (in the sense of Bayesian updating) in favor of these ideas, causing them to gain support among the pivotal moderates and by 1775 the moderates had switched sides to support the radicals in revolution against the British.

The reemergence of order after the revolution was fundamentally dependent on the heritage of the colonial era. The set of political and economic rules of the game that were established with British rule provided for self-government of the colonies and well specified property rights in the economic sphere. Controversies abounded during the era of the Articles of Confederation and the establishment of the Constitution, but the foundations of stability of political and economic rules were carried over to independence from the colonial charters. The principles of political order discussed above were reflected in the way the Constitution lowered the stakes of national political action by instituting a complex system of enumerated powers, a separation of powers system, and a system of federalism placing striking limits on the national government. The debates during this era served to provide new shared beliefs about the bounds on the national government and the importance of citizen rights and state autonomy.

Competition among the states in the face of a growing common market gave states the incentive to foster a favorable economic climate, and the presence of a hard budget constraint greatly limited the ability of the states to subsidize local economic agents. Citizens in the early American republic favored freedom for state and local governments and thus strong limits on national government. The widely held belief system combined with the political institutions, property rights, and law produced a system highly favorable to decentralized competitive markets. When the system was combined with the favorable factor endowments that the country inherited, the result was rapid economic development.

The Civil War was a terrible disruption in the history of the United States brought on by a breakdown in the political stalemate that had preserved the Union through growing political, economic, and social conflict between the North and South. In effect the mechanisms that had provided credible commitment to both sides disappeared with that breakdown, thereby convincing Southern states that secession was the only viable alternative.[5] The war was one of the most devastating in history but the remarkable feature in terms of the subject of this chapter was the extraordinary recovery. Within a few years after the end of the war economic growth was renewed in the North and before the end of the century in the South as well, though the end of reconstruction in 1877 resulted in perpetuation of second class citizenship for African Americans through much of the twentieth century. But political, economic, and social order did ensue and not only produced sustained economic growth through that century but via political and social institutional change dramatically improved the status of African Americans as well.

The adaptively efficient institutional structure that has characterized the American economy is a consequence of path dependence (the political and economic institutions inherited from British rule), favorable factor endowments (boundless rich land and resources, immigration

---

[5] For a more detailed analytical account see Weingast (1998).

of labor and capital from Europe), endless favorable events throughout the nineteenth century that reinforced the belief system that supported the formal political and economic institutions (such as the widespread discovery of gold at the end of the nineteenth century which produced prosperity for agriculture after decades of discontent), and good luck (the anti-federalist boycott of the constitutional convention for example). One critical fact should be emphasized. The heritage of British institutions created a favorable milieu for the development of the institutions of impersonal exchange which were the foundation of the long-term economic growth of the American economy.

V

The Latin American story starts with Spanish (and Portuguese) colonization of the new world. The entire pattern of settlement, trade, and development was geared to the extraction of precious metals for the Crown. It was an authoritarian system ruled from Madrid. Neither self-government nor competitive markets existed. The Crown granted exclusive monopoly privileges to selected merchants and trade was confined to a small number of ports in the whole of South America. The objective of the Spanish mercantilist structure was to implement the movement of precious metals to Spain, not to promote the development of Latin America. Such a pattern of settlement and extractive economic policies had profound implications for Latin America after independence.

Napoleon's imprisonment of the Spanish King in 1807 led to efforts to redefine the colonies' relationship to the metropolis and initiated the outbreak of independence movements throughout Spanish America. The defeat of Spanish armies resulted in the fragmentation of the former colonies into new republics. Many of these adapted a version of the United States Constitution as a model for independence, but the consequences were radically different. Without the heritage of colonial self-government and well-specified property rights, independence disintegrated into a violent struggle among competing groups for control of the polity and economy. Capturing the polity and using it as a vehicle of personal exchange in all markets was the result. In most of Spanish

America it took a half century for one of the competing groups to emerge victorious. Establishing order became a goal in itself, thus creating and perpetuating authoritarian regimes—the phenomenon of "caudillismo" became pervasive.

The demise of the colonial system raised new conflicts that the newly created states were unable to resolve. Attempts to create new republican institutions (U.S.-inspired constitutions) clashed with the political foundations of the old order. Under the royal system, rights were granted to individuals and groups based on personal ties to the Crown. The result was huge land grants to wealthy individuals and the church; rights and privileges to the military; and a series of local monopolies in production and trade. Self-government was completely absent. Personal ties dominated political and economic exchange. With independence, deep political conflicts emerged with those who had inherited rights from the royal regime in fundamental conflict with the republican institutions and consequent organizations that evolved with independence.

The discussion of sources of disorder gives us a handle to understand the Spanish American ex-colonies after independence. There was no shared belief system about the role of government, the state, corporate privileges, and citizenship. There was, however, a common set of beliefs built on personal exchange which fostered strong personal relationships but undercut the construction of institutions of impersonal exchange. The absence of consensus about the legitimate ends of government and how society should be organized resulted in failure to police limits to the state. The absence of agreement about basic political structure combined with an absence of a shared belief system resulted in an absence of credible commitment by the new states and in inherent political instability.

Yet inherent political instability did not completely halt economic growth. In Latin America it produced neither economic collapse nor stagnation but continuing instability, extensive rent seeking, political authoritarianism, adverse income distribution, and an inefficient provision of public goods, with slow economic growth. In Mexico, for example, vertical political integration consisted of a coalition of government, asset holders, and a third party that could credibly commit the parties to uphold agreements. While a third party could be a foreign state, in

Mexico it was a domestic group whose support was essential to the government and who derived rents from the asset holders. The result was not a universal protection of property rights but a selective protection confined to the relevant asset holders.[6] This account of Mexico has wide applicability not only to Latin America but with variation to much third world history. It is important to note that it cannot be in the interest of politically dominant groups to stop all growth as doing so would dry up the sources of income. What Mancur Olson described as the stationary bandit model is one in which such a player has an essential stake in not confiscating all of the net income of asset holders (McGuire and Olson 1996).

Two centuries after independence the historical contrast between North America and Latin America continues to provide the underlying basis for the contrasting performance. The United States retains a robust system of federalism, democracy, limited government, and thriving markets. Much of Latin America is still characterized by stop-and-go development, fragile democratic institutions, questionable foundations of citizen rights, personal exchange, and monopolized markets.[7] Some of the contrasting performance can be explained by standard factor endowments analysis from neo-classical economics. Endowments were clearly a driving force in the pattern of European colonization. But the endowments argument must be fundamentally supplemented by the powerful consequences of the path dependent results of colonial inheritance, the institutions of slavery and the encomienda system, and contrasting institutional evolutions that occurred as a consequence of this blend of economic and institutional forces over the two centuries. The source of these contrasting institutional patterns was the fundamental beliefs of the key players in each case. The evolution of the belief system in Britain will be explored in chapter 10. That belief system, carried over to the American colonies, provided the basic source of the adaptively efficient institutions that evolved. In contrast,

---

[6] See Haber et al. (2003).

[7] Nowhere is this fragility better illustrated than in the history of Argentina—a country with the sixth highest income per capita in the world in 1940 and then stagnation for more than forty years followed by brief revival and (as of this writing) economic collapse. For a discussion of the sources of erosion of Argentine prosperity see Alston and Gallo (2001).

the beliefs underlying the institutions promulgated by the Spanish Crown have provided two centuries of instability, turmoil, personal exchange, and limited development.

Order and disorder have their foundation in the institutional structure that has evolved over time. While societies will, at times, undergo periods of disorder as a result of the crises that beset societies in a world of continuous change, those societies with a heritage of stable institutions will recover rapidly in contrast to those without such a heritage.

Getting It Right and Getting It Wrong

WHEN HUMANS understand their environment as reflected in their beliefs and construct an institutional framework that enables them to implement their desired objectives, then there is consistency between the objectives of those players in a position to shape their destiny and the desired outcomes. We could conceive of the enormous increase in life expectancy and material well-being of the past several centuries as reflecting such consistency. But this improvement has been a trial and error process of change with lots of errors, endless losers, and no guarantee that we will continue to get it right in spite of the enormous accretion of knowledge over those centuries. Indeed human history is a sobering testimonial to the fallibility of humans in the face of ubiquitous uncertainty. The reason should be clear from the foregoing chapters. We are continually altering our environment in new ways (and there are also non-manmade alterations), and there is no guarantee that we will understand correctly the changes in the environment, develop the appropriate institutions, and implement policies to solve the new problems we will face. A review of the stringent conditions for getting it right in a dynamic setting should make clear why this is so.

Getting it right through time means that we perceive correctly changes in the human environment, incorporate those perceptions in our belief system, and alter the institutions accordingly. Doing so would entail that

1. the implications of the novel changes would be understood with respect to the effects on the three fundamental sources of change—demography, the stock of knowledge, and institutions—and the resultant new interaction among them;

2. this new knowledge would be incorporated in the belief systems of those in a position to modify the institutional matrix;

3. the formal rules, the informal constraints, and the enforcement characteristics would be altered accordingly and would produce the desired
changes in societal performance.

At stake in such contexts are two issues about which we know all too
little: how humans make decisions in the face of strong uncertainty,
and how humans learn. These have been the subject of chapters 3 and
4. Here I wish to elaborate on three critical points in human decision
making where we have tended—or do or will tend—to get it wrong.
The first two concern the process of change at the macro level: how in
the face of truly novel situations do societies evolve, and what kind of
beliefs best prepare them to deal with the novelty. The third concerns
change at the more micro level: what adjustments of factor and product
markets are necessary to maintain economic efficiency in the context
of changing technology, organization, and external environment.

I

We tend to get it wrong when the accumulated experiences and beliefs
derived from the past do not provide a correct guide to future decision
making. There are two reasons. The set of mental models, categories,
and classifications of the neural networks that have evolved in our belief
system through which the new evidence gets filtered have no existing
patterns that can correctly assess the new evidence. And in cases where
conflicting beliefs have evolved, the dominant organizations (and their
entrepreneurs) may view the necessary changes as a threat to their survival. To the degree that the entrepreneurs of such organizations control
decision making they can thwart the necessary changes. The first of
these factors stems from our not correctly comprehending what is hap-
pening to us; the second, from an inability to make the necessary institutional adjustments.

The shift from personal to impersonal exchange has produced just
such a stumbling block both historically and in the contemporary
world. Personal exchange relies on reciprocity, repeat dealings, and the
kind of informal norms that tend to evolve from strong reciprocity
relationships. Impersonal exchange requires the development of eco-

nomic and political institutions that alter the pay-offs in exchange to reward cooperative behavior. The creation of the necessary institutions requires a fundamental alteration in the structure of the economy and the polity which frequently is not in the feasible set given the historically derived beliefs and institutions of the players. The unique development of the Western world from relative backwardness in the tenth century to world hegemony by the eighteenth gives us a glimpse of the kind of historical evolution that made such a change possible. A number of studies have explored the evolution of such institutions in the rise of the Western world (for example, Milgrom et al. 1990; Greif 1993 and forthcoming a). Successful evolution has entailed radical alteration in economic institutions in order to make such long distance and impersonal trade viable. Avner Greif explores an intermediate step in this process in pre-modern Europe that facilitated the transformation: in the Community Responsibility System common knowledge regarding social structure could take advantage of intra-community, personal contract enforcement to support inter-community impersonal exchange (Greif forthcoming b).

The economic institutions must ultimately be undergirded by political institutions. The Community Responsibility System (Greif forthcoming b), by fostering the growth of long distance trade and community size, put pressure on the economic system and encouraged the state to step in to provide for legal enforcement of contracts. But there is nothing automatic about the creation of the essential political institutions that will, in fact, create and enforce the necessary legal system. North and Weingast (1989) explore this process in the case of the Glorious Revolution in England in 1689. That study details the curtailment in the autocratic powers of the monarchy and development of parliament—a major step in the development of representative government. The most careful, and suggestive, study of this transformation has been made by Avner Greif (1994b), who compares the evolving structure of political and economic institutions of Genoese traders, which ultimately provided the essential institutions for impersonal exchange, and the practices of the Mahgribi traders (Jewish merchants but in a Muslim culture), who fail to make the necessary institutional adjustments and lose out in the competitive trade of the Mediterranean.

The widespread failure in the modern world of political institutions that will put in place and enforce effective legal systems making possible low cost enforcement of contracts makes clear that we have a way to go in understanding the process of creating the essential political institutions. Latin American experience is replete with instances of unstable political institutions leading to recurring military dictatorships; sub-Saharan African polities have been a disastrous source of falling per capita income for much of the past several decades.

The analysis in preceding chapters enables us to pinpoint the sources of the inability to shift rapidly from personal to impersonal exchange:

1. The genetic architecture that evolved from our three million years as hunter/gatherers was geared to a world of small group interaction which predisposed us to engage in the kind of small-scale cooperative behavior that characterized clan, tribe, and other small group interactions necessary for survival in a hostile physical environment. That genetic architecture did prepare us for personal exchange. It did not prepare us for a world of impersonal exchange. Indeed "defection" was the "natural" response.

2. Overcoming this natural response, to defect, entailed the development of mental constructs that could visualize the consequences of a world in which there were favorable pay-offs to impersonal exchange. Such novel situations required a gradual "indoctrination" into increasingly impersonal relationships in order for the players to perceive and adopt the appropriate institutions.

3. But it is not enough to perceive the feasibility of the appropriate economic institutions and organizations—such as bills of exchange, banks, corporate structures, firms, and various economic institutions engaged in long distance trade—also necessary was the development of impersonal enforcement mechanisms to provide effective enforcement of agreements in impersonal exchange. Ultimately that entailed the development of the state as the source of coercive authority.

4. The establishment of a state with the coercive ability to enforce property rights (at low cost) results in a state with the ability to use that coercive authority to exploit its citizens, as Madison reminded us a long time ago. Creating a strong but limited polity is still a long way from being completely understood even though we have made progress in understanding the is-

sues. But one fact is clear; such a state cannot be created overnight. It entails the development of effective informal norms of behavior that will undergird formal rules.

II

The Western world evolved from a simple world of personal exchange to the complex interdependent world that characterizes the developed economies today. Economic historians have typically described it in terms of growth in the size of markets until today we glibly talk about a global economy. Just how does it work? Sociologists looking empirically at information networks describe an immensely complicated communications structure that pulls the dispersed knowledge together in order to use it effectively in the growth of productivity of the modern economy. As the Western world evolved, the process of change was a gradual accretion of an ever more comprehensive price system supplemented, complemented, and sometimes obstructed by the accretion of political rules and regulations which were only occasionally deliberately enacted to effectuate more efficient combinations of knowledge. The Western world has had a long gestation period to work out the interconnections to make markets work more efficiently (the subject of the next section) although still far from ideally. But developing countries face a far more daunting task. To survive and grow in the context of the competition from the already developed world, they must deliberately construct an effective price system and supplement it by creating the institutions and organizations to integrate that knowledge at low costs of transacting. Standard economic theory is no help as a guide. It would imply that someone from a developing economy who acquired the advanced knowledge in say chemistry would command a wage commensurate with the relative scarcity of such knowledge in a developing country and therefore automatically provide the correct incentives to resolve the problem. In fact that person will command a far higher wage in a developed economy. It is only when that specialized knowledge can get integrated with other complementary knowledge at low cost that it is very valuable.

The interconnections necessary to combine distributed knowledge effectively entail much more than an effective price system, although that is an essential prerequisite. The essential public goods, asymmetric information, and ubiquitous externalities require that institutions and organizations be created to integrate this dispersed knowledge at low cost of transacting. We are still some distance from knowing completely the steps along the way,[1] but they may be stated as follows:

1. In a world of autarchy individuals had to be jacks of all trades. Survival depended on acquiring the knowledge to deal with the variety of problems essential to survival. In such a context increased specialization would be at the expense of the variety necessary for survival.

2. As increased specialization occurred with the growth of markets, individuals exchanged increased specialized knowledge at the expense of less "general" knowledge. That loss in general knowledge had to be made up by trade.

3. Trade will make the individual better off only if the increased uncertainty due to specialization is more than compensated for by the reduction in uncertainty resulting from the availability of wider variety.

4. There is nothing automatic about such a reduction in uncertainty. It entails low costs of transacting across these other markets. Goods (and services) must be designed in such a way that the new user does not have to have the detailed knowledge of the specialist. We do not expect the purchaser of a car to be a mechanic or engineer nor the user of a computer to be a computer programmer. Warranties, guarantees, trade marks are just illustrations of the vast range of institutions and organizations that enabled specialized individuals to have access to the other consumer markets that they needed in order to take advantage of the potential economies possible in such a world of specialization.

5. An even more complex structure is essential for producers to integrate productive knowledge, as the study of information networks attests. Germany pioneered in the application of scientific principles to technology in the chemical industry in the nineteenth century. But it is in the United States where this fusion has been developed in universities, beginning with the first curriculum of Chemical Engineering at MIT in 1888. Combining

---

[1] This issue is elaborated in much more detail in Martens (2004).

chemical knowledge with engineering principles produced revolutionary developments.[2] American universities today are at the heart of the revolutionary integration of pure and applied knowledge in every field of development. Silicon Valley is only one illustration, but a spectacular one, of the fruits of such integration. Other parts of the developed world have lagged behind in this integration; and the creation of the necessary institutions and organizations in the less developed world is a major challenge.

III

Economists of a libertarian persuasion have for some time labored under the delusion that there is something called laissez faire and that once there are in place "efficient" property rights and the rule of law the economy will perform well without further adjustment. The scandals involving Enron, Dynegy, WorldCom, and others in 2001–2002 should have laid such a delusion to rest. In fact, not only must factor and product markets be structured at *a moment of time* to get the players to compete via price and quality (rather than by killing each other or engaging in other kinds of anti-social activities) but the conditions for maintaining market efficiency will vary *over time* with changes in technology, human capital, market conditions, and information costs. Each factor and product market is characterized by a structure that defines the margins at which the players can operate to affect the profitability of their operation. Transaction costs—here measurement and enforcement costs—will vary in each case; in order to reduce such costs there must be an institutional structure that will provide incentives for the players to compete at those margins, and those margins alone, that will be socially productive. Typically this entails a set of formal (usually a mixture of laws, rules, and regulations) and informal constraints to produce the desired results. Let us see if we can pinpoint the problems associated with creating "efficient" markets at a moment of time and then the additional problems that change over time poses for maintaining efficient markets. First at a moment of time:

[2] See Rosenberg and Birdzell (1986, chapter 8).

1. While the utility function of players in every market will vary we can nevertheless assume that income and wealth maximization (with the usual caveats about making choices in a world of uncertainty) will guide the choices of the players, subject to the constraints on the players imposed by the state of technology and the competitive conditions. But a combination of these two variables produces an immense variety of margins at which the players can and will act. What we seek to know is what set of incentives and disincentives will provide the players in each factor and product market with the correct inducements.

2. The performance characteristics of each market will be a consequence of both the formal rules and the informal norms of behavior that modify, qualify, or even negate the formal rules. The transaction costs in each market will reflect the combination of formal and informal constraints. Even when property rights are well specified, both measurement and enforcement will be imperfect since the property rights will provide general rules rather than "cater" to the specific characteristics of each market.

3. Additional specific rules for each market will be made by a government that is hardly a disinterested party. The structure of political markets will determine whose voices are "heard" in shaping additional rules governing each market.

4. Even when the ostensible objective of government policy is economic efficiency it is not obvious that the government players will possess sufficient economic sophistication to achieve that objective.

5. Enforcement will be made by agents—whether regulatory bodies or courts—with their own agenda.

Now over time: Not only does each factor and product market require different specific constraints so that it will provide the right incentive structure for the players, but economic change will require continual alteration in the institutional structure in order to maintain efficiency. This is particularly critical for capital markets, which however well they may serve to facilitate growth at one time, may become obstacles to growth at another time; and there is no guarantee that they will automatically evolve as the economy evolves. The structure of the market will determine the incentives of the players and with changes in the aforementioned conditions the incentives that at time t would induce the players to make an efficient capital market may in time $t + 1$

induce the players to engage in activities that undermine, weaken, or indeed destroy the capital market with consequent adverse effects on the economy as a whole. The history of Japan in the 1990s is a classic instance of a capital market that initially fueled extraordinary development—that of post–World War II—only to develop the sclerosis that followed. As with capital markets, so too with other markets in a world of dynamic change.

The problem is complex because successful adaptation to changing conditions entails altering economic institutions, which frequently entails the enactment through the polity of new rules. To the degree that the players (that is, entrepreneurs of economic organizations) perceive the need for adaptation they may be in a position to make the necessary alterations themselves. Something like that appears to characterize the successful adaptation of American firms in automobiles, steel, and software to Japanese competition in the 1980s, which led in the 1990s to successful organizational innovation in American firms. But when change involves the polity and the political enactment of new rules, the adaptation is much less likely to be forthcoming. The polity becomes the battleground for those who believe they would be adversely affected by the rule changes. In the case of Japan's capital market, the inability of the polity and specifically the Ministry of Finance to restructure this market was the immediate source of the sclerosis. But history is replete with illustrations of failure to alter the rules in the face of changing conditions. Mancur Olson's *The Rise and Decline of Nations* (1982) studies the inherent tendency of markets to develop sclerosis over time in the absence of "revolutionary institutional change."

Neo-classical economists have generally come to perceive that institutions are important and that an underpinning of property rights and the rule of law are necessary conditions for a successful economy. That is a big improvement in their perceptions and together with a recognition of the importance of macro stability has led to improved advice by both international organizations and economic advisors. But such advice is clearly insufficient in the dynamic world we live in. There is little evidence that these advisors and international organizations properly perceive the need for ongoing institutional change as the fundamental characteristics of a particular efficient market are altered. Capital markets appear to be the most sensitive to ongoing need for alteration as economies evolve and the history of economic crises is replete with stories of the critical role of financial markets in such events. Yet there are few systematic studies of the institutional adjustments necessary for dynamically efficient capital markets;[3] nor have such studies been made with respect to other factor and product markets.

Prolonged failure to improve individual factor and product markets can lead to and has led to declining overall rates of growth and indeed stagnation. We have looked at Japan; the destruction of the export market for agricultural goods in Argentina after 1940 led to forty years of relative decline in that economy. It will be useful to specify the issues involved with maintaining efficient markets over time:

1. Alterations in the performance characteristics of a market require an initial understanding of the source(s) of such change.

2. "Successful" alterations designed to improve market performance require the correct theory of the overall process of change.

3. Implementing that correct theory entails that the key players (that is entrepreneurs in a position to alter that market structure) possess such theory and are willing and able to act upon it.

4. Where the alterations entail changes that must be enacted by the polity, there is an additional hurdle in enacting such political policies. This additional hurdle is that the existing institutional structure will have spawned organizations with a stake in that existing institutional structure and such organizations will attempt to thwart the changes.

IV

Neo-classical economic theory is static and as a consequence has tended to produce blinders on policy makers deriving their inspiration from that theory. The result is all too frequently policy prescriptions that produce results at odds with intentions because policy derived from static theory in a dynamic setting is going to produce unanticipated (and unpleasant) outcomes. By now it should be clear that no dynamic theory of change is advanced in this study and I hope that it is equally

---

[3] A suggestive study is by Stiglitz et al. (1998).

clear that no such theory that could be useful is likely to evolve. While evolutionary game theory may capture some interesting elements of a particular change, generalization would render it so unwieldy as to be of little value. However, specifying why such a general theory is unlikely should prepare us for a more limited but manageable approach to dealing with dynamic change. The building blocks for such an approach have been implicit or explicit in earlier chapters. Specifically:

1. Leaving aside change that can be induced by alterations in the physical environment, changes in the human environment will broadly mirror the changes in institutions that are the subject of the concluding section of chapter 5. They will have as their source the underlying beliefs of those organizational entrepreneurs (political, social, and economic) in a position to enact alterations in the institutional environment. So far so good.

2. But the next step is more difficult. Such initial changes can alter the perceived opportunity costs of complementary or substitute organizations. We would have to have detailed understanding of the complex interdependent institutional matrix to unravel those connections. We would also have to know the new opportunity costs of the affected organizations. Economics and political economy have not devoted resources to understanding the complex interdependent character of market structures so as to be self-conscious about the secondary consequences of an initial change. If, for example, a change in a law promoted by a business firm adversely affected the viability of a trade union we would need to know the effective political "clout" of the trade union in obstructing or preventing or repealing such an action. Understanding the structure of the polity would be essential to predicting the outcome.

3. More detailed knowledge than we currently possess of the institutional structure of an economy is needed so that we are aware of the existing institutional matrix and therefore are self-conscious about the interconnections. The information network analysis being undertaken by sociologists, while itself a-theoretical, would be a major step in getting a better grasp of that matrix. Once we have undertaken such studies we are in a position to perceive the alterations in the opportunity costs of affected organizations and take that information into account in making policies. That hardly qualifies as anything like dealing with dynamic change properly; but it does make us more conscious of the issues we must deal with.

The Rise of the Western World

THE RISE of the Western world was the ascendancy of a relatively backward part of the world to world hegemony between the tenth and the eighteenth centuries.[1] It involved economic, political, and military changes as well as a shift in the focus of institutional change—from dealing with the uncertainties associated with the physical environment to dealing with those of the increasingly complex human environment. The rise of science and its systematic application to solving problems not only of economic scarcity but also of human well-being was still in its infancy by the eighteenth century but the foundation had been laid for the revolutionary developments of the next two centuries. This chapter concentrates on that foundation as illustrative of the overall process of change in society. Examined in other chapters are such important issues as the movement from personal to impersonal exchange and the integration of distributed knowledge as well as those involved in devising efficient markets. Here we concentrate on the complex interplay among beliefs, institutions, and other factors such as geography, military technology, and evolving competitive conditions that influenced the process of change. Of necessity, therefore, the chapter goes into more detailed description than do other chapters.

I

Since history is about how yesterday's choices affect today's decisions, any starting point is not just arbitrary but does violence to the essential continuity of history. If we begin our story with northwest Europe of the tenth century we do so, therefore, with a glance over our shoulder at the background sources of that landscape.

[1] This chapter is drawn from North (1995b).

The Roman Empire disappeared in the chaotic conditions of the fifth century A.D; a more or less arbitrary historical chronology dates the end of feudalism about a millenium later, in 1500. In between these dates western Europe gradually emerged from the anarchy that followed the collapse of Roman order and the overrunning of western Europe by Germanic tribes, to develop the political and economic structure which set the scene for subsequent developments. This evolution was basically conditioned by the heritage of Greco-Roman civilization which persisted (particularly in southern Europe), modifying and ultimately shaping many of the institutional arrangements that emerged in the sixth to the tenth centuries. The manor appears to be a lineal descendent of the Roman villa and the dependent coloni a predecessor of the serf of the feudal world. Slavery, too, continued into the Middle Ages. Roman law continued and where order evolved served as the basis for the development of property rights.

The Church carried over the cultural heritage of the classical world to the Middle Ages. It was the lonely repository of learning—and indeed monasteries were frequently the most efficient farming centers of medieval Europe. If the Church was a major possessor of material wealth, selling salvation in return for treasure and land, it was also characterized by asceticism, hermit life, and devout missionaries. Most important, it provided a unified belief structure, an ideological frame of reference, that shaped perceptions in the medieval world. This common frame of reference served as the basis for the ongoing evolution of perceptions that would guide choices shaping the future of polities and economies.

Northwest Europe was a geographic contrast to the Mediterranean rim, the seat of Greco-Roman civilization. The latter was characterized by light and/or seasonal rainfall, light soils, and a varied agriculture ranging from viticulture and olive trees to cereals; the former by abundant rainfall, thick forests, and heavy soils that suited it to livestock and, with appropriate modifications of ploughs, cereal production. These climatic and geographic features determined the agrarian structure of the economies of northwest Europe.

These institutional, intellectual, and geographic background conditions of tenth-century life in northwest Europe must be set in the context of the most fundamental initial organizational condition—the lack of large-scale economic and political order. The disintegration of the Roman Empire presaged more than half-a-millenium of small-scale political units. Whatever advantages had existed in large-scale political-economic organization were absent or severely diluted in the era that followed. The Roman Empire persisted in the east until Constantinople was taken by the Turks in 1453; and the Muslim world built on the charismatic faith of the new religion created an empire spreading over North Africa and into Europe. But neither these exceptions nor the short-lived Carolingian Empire refute the critical point that the conditions that had made possible a single empire governing the Mediterranean world had disappeared.

Assault from three directions, by Vikings, Magyars, and Muslims, imposed its stamp on the region. Vikings appeared off the coast of England in 786, off Ireland in 795, and off Gaul in 799. London was sacked in 841; Viking longboats moved up navigable rivers to attack such diverse towns as Rouen in the north and Toulouse in the south. Hungarian horsemen raided Bremen in 915 and reached as far west as Orleans in 937. The viable response was the fixed fortification, the heavily armored knight, and the hierarchical, decentralized structure of feudalism. The military result was something of a stalemate. The castle was impregnable to all but the most persistent—and well-financed—opposition that could undertake the siege necessary to starve out the inhabitants; warfare was typically small scale between heavily armored knights. The Vikings were repulsed at the siege of Paris in 885 and the Magyars were defeated near Augsburg in 995. In consequence there was a revival of local order, an expansion of manors—ones being carved out of the wilderness—and a growth of towns. And it is in the context of these initial conditions that the interplay between political, economic, and military changes initiated the unique conditions that led to sustained economic growth.

Economic activity took place within the manor (with some exceptions) and in towns. Manorial organization was typified by a threefold division of land into the lord's demesne, the peasant holdings, and the commons. The majority of peasants were bound to the manor as serfs owing labor services (two or three days a week) and dues to the lord of the manor. They were subject to the lord's jurisdiction, had to seek justice in the lord's court, and were restricted in their movements and in their economic transactions (Preirte-Orton 1960, 424–25). Traditional manorial organization provided scant encouragement for economic growth. The isolation of the manor inhibited specialization and division of labor and slowed the diffusion of technology when it did develop. The incentives imbedded in the customs of the manor provided little impetus for the rapid growth of skills and knowledge or technological change. The heavy plough with wheels, moldboard, and colter; the horsecollar; and the horseshoe did make their appearance although the shift from oxen to horses came mostly after the ninth century and then only slowly (Mokyr 1990, chapter 3). Likewise the shift from the two-field to the three-field system of crop rotation was a very gradual change. But population was growing at least from the tenth century on, most likely as a result of the relative improvements in order that followed the end of the incursions of Vikings and Magyars. This population growth—as well as subsequent decline—would play a major role in altering the manorial organization.

The evolving towns were the centers of rapid economic—and political—change in response to the improved establishment of order over larger areas. Whether the numerous city republics of north and central Italy or the urban centers that grew up in the Low Countries in the tenth century, they were sources of dynamic changes resulting from the opportunities of expanding trade in the Mediterranean or the basins of the Scheldt and the Meuse and the ties to both south Europe and the Baltic and North Sea coastal areas.

Prior to 1300 trade was carried on primarily by traveling merchants. Such traders often formed societies for mutual protection; some of these even required their members to be suitably armed when traveling in caravans, indicating that problems of peace and order had not been completely settled. The importance of traveling merchants—and of fairs—began to decline after 1300 (De Roover 1965). The growth of trade fueled the growth of towns and the settlement of merchants further accelerated their development. The constraints imposed by geography and the high costs of land transport dictated the urban locations: at the head of a gulf (Bruges), where a road crossed a river (Maestricht), near the confluence of two rivers (Ghent), or at a breakpoint in transportation (Brussels).

II

The tenth to the sixteenth century in northwest Europe was a period of endless warfare at every level, from the local conflicts of barons to the relatively large-scale battles of the Hundred Years War. It was also an era of radical demographic change, with population growth from the tenth to the fourteenth centuries and then the decline beginning in the early fourteenth century that probably persisted for 150 years before being reversed.

Changes in military technology led to profound changes not only in the nature of warfare but in the viable size of political units (Bean 1973). Warfare became more costly both because of the costs of training disciplined units and because of the increased capital costs of the offensive and defensive equipment. Whether the result was the dangerous employment of skilled mercenaries or the initiation of a professional standing army by Charles VII of France, political units needed more revenue to survive than could be obtained from a sovereign "living on his own" from traditional feudal sources. Yet if the fiscal needs of the sovereign had increased, the potential resources to generate additional revenue in the economies had also increased. The establishment of order over larger areas resulted in profound changes in population, the growth of trade, the expansion of markets, and the widespread development of money economies.

In the fourteenth century there was a precipitous decline in urban populations as a consequence of the bubonic and pneumonic plagues. The immediate consequence was an absolute decline in the volume of trade and commerce and in the revenue available to be taxed or appropriated by princes. But the decline in commerce was not equal to that in population. The basic institutional structure of rules and laws persisted and provided the essential framework that would serve as the basis of growth when population revived. Population decline had a more fundamental impact on agrarian organization. It led to a change in the land/man ratio that made labor scarce and forced an increased competition among landlords, which ultimately altered the organization of the manor and of agriculture.

The revenue necessary to fiscally strapped rulers could be confiscated, could be borrowed (particularly from Florentine bankers), or could be traded by constituent economic groups in return for services provided by the sovereign. All these methods were tried. Confiscation killed the goose that laid the golden egg. Eventually Florentine (and other) bankers were burned by repudiation—but not before monarchs had been supported in expensive wars and some bankers had realized handsome profits from Crown monopolies and other favors from rulers. The third method, the exchange of services—particularly the granting and enforcing of property rights—for revenue, produced a wide variety of structural changes, from the protection of alien merchants, to the incorporation of guild and merchant law into legal codes and enforcement by the state, to the establishment of Parliament, Estates General, and Cortes.

III

The implications of these military and demographic/economic changes for institutional and organizational change were profound. The economic changes in agriculture were away from the self-sufficient manor with dependent labor toward a market-oriented agriculture of landlords and peasants bound together less by customary rights and obligations and more by an evolving structure of property rights.

The growth of towns and cities around an expanding national and international commerce was made possible by a number of institutional and organizational innovations. The evolution of the bill of exchange and the development of techniques for negotiability and discounting required the development of centers where such events could occur—the Champagne and other fairs, banks, and eventually financial houses that would specialize in discounting. Marine insurance evolved from sporadic individual contracts covering partial payment for losses to standard printed contracts offered by specialized firms. Marine insurance was one way to spread risks; another was business organization that permitted either portfolio diversification or the aggregation of a number of investors such as the commenda, the regulated company, and finally the joint stock company (North 1991). The mechanisms for contract enforcement appear to have had their beginnings in internal codes of conduct of fraternal orders of guild merchants, which were enforced by the threat of ostracism. These codes evolved into merchant law and spread throughout the European trading area; gradually they became integrated with common and Roman law and enforcement was eventually taken over by the state (Milgrom et al. 1990).

The last point is critical. The economic institutional structure was made possible by the evolution of polities that eventually provided a framework of law and its enforcement. Such a framework is an essential requirement for the impersonal exchange that is necessary for economic growth. The development was a long process of (some) polities gradually shifting from extortion to trading "protection and justice" for revenue. The initial impetus for this development was the desperate search for additional revenue; but as noted above, obtaining revenue could take several forms—confiscation or debt repudiation on the one hand or the trading of property rights and their enforcement for revenue on the other.

Radically different results ensued from the divergent policies of rulers in the face of fiscal crises but one constant was the gradual emergence of the nation state, whether in the context of the economic growth that characterized the Netherlands or of the stagnation that ensued from Spanish policies.

To understand the success of the Netherlands one must look back at the evolution of prosperous towns of the Low Countries such as Bruges, Ghent, and Liege; their internal conflicts; and their relationship to Burgundian and Habsburg rule. The prosperity of the towns, whether based on the wool cloth trade or metals trade, early on made for an urban-centered, market-oriented area unique at a time of overwhelmingly rural societies. Their internal conflicts reflected ongoing tensions between patrician and crafts and persistent conflict over ongoing efforts to create local monopolies which, when successful, led to a drying up of the very sources of productivity which had been the mainspring of their growth. The overall impact of the advent of Burgundian control was to discourage restrictive practices. In 1463 Philip the Good created a representative body, the States General, which enacted laws and had the authority to vote taxes for the ruler. This assembly encouraged the growth of trade and commerce. The Burgundian (and later Habsburg) rulers themselves, in spite of vigorous opposition, actively discouraged monopoly privileges embodied in guild and trade restrictions such as those in the cloth towns of Bruges and Ghent. The rulers were supported by new centers of industry that sprang up in response to the favorable incentives embodied in the rules and property rights. The Burgundians and Habsburgs were rewarded by a level of prosperity that generated tax revenues that made the Low Countries the jewel in the Habsburg Empire. Eventually the ever more exacting revenue demands of Philip II led to revolt, the sacking of Antwerp, the successful separation of the seven northern provinces, and the rise to commercial supremacy of Amsterdam. And it was in the Netherlands and Amstersdam specifically that modern economic growth had its genesis.

Contrast this brief story of economic growth with that of Spain. Ferdinand and Isabella united Castile and Aragon to form a nation state after centuries of strife with the Moors and ceaseless internal wars among feudal barons. When Charles V ascended the throne in 1516 the great era of Spanish hegemony over Europe was initiated. It was characterized by prosperity with growing fiscal revenues from Aragon, Naples, Milan, and particularly the Low Countries. Increased revenues were matched by increased expenditures as Charles V maintained the largest and best equipped army in Europe. Maintaining and expanding the Empire, however, was ever more costly; and when the Low Countries revolted against Charles V's successor, Philip II, the result was not only to lose a major source of revenue but to incur the additional expenses of war with the seven provinces. The fiscal crisis deepened as treasure from the New World declined. The desperate search for revenue led to granting local monopolies for revenue, to confiscations, and to ever higher rates of domestic taxation. The predictable results were a decline of trade and commerce as well as numerous bankruptcies of the state.

These contrasting stories of economic growth and decline have been, with appropriate but usually minor modification, repeated endlessly in history and in the modern world. Growth has been generated when the economy has provided institutional incentives to undertake productivity-raising activities such as the Dutch undertook. Decline has resulted from disincentives to engage in productive activity as a consequence of centralized political control of the economy and monopoly privileges. The failures vastly exceed the successes. Economic growth has been the

THE RISE OF THE WESTERN WORLD

exception; stagnation and decline have been the rule, reflecting a persistent tendency toward failure in human organization. Let us now turn to the evolution of beliefs that guide human choices and actions.

IV

In his *Protestant Ethic and the Spirit of Capitalism*, Max Weber is concerned to show that the religious ethic embodied in Protestantism—and specifically Calvinism—contained values that promoted the growth of capitalism. But which way does the causation run; and how do we know that both the values and the growth of capitalism did not stem from some other source (Tawney 1926)? Weber makes a connection between religious views and values, and between values and economic behavior; but he does not demonstrate how the consequent behavior would generate the growth of the specific institutions and organizations that produced a growing economic system (Coleman 1990, 6). Moreover Counter-Reformation Catholicism may have equally encouraged the same individualism and sense of discipline that Weber uniquely ascribes to Protestantism.

It will be useful to consider the relationship between behavioral beliefs and the evolution of specific institutional and organizational structures because this approach provides an explanation for such evolution. A long-standing view of many scholars has been that individualistic behavioral beliefs are congenial to economic growth. Alan Macfarlane's controversial *The Origins of English Individualism* traces the sources of English individualism back to the thirteenth century or earlier. It paints a picture of a fluid, individualistically oriented set of attitudes toward the family, the organization of work, and the social structure of the village community. These attitudes were manifested in a set of formal rules dealing with property inheritance and the legal status of women. We have already looked at Avner Greif's study (1989, 1994a) comparing Genoese traders with traders who had adopted the cultural and social attributes of Islamic society in the Mediterranean trade of the eleventh and twelfth centuries. He detects systematic differences in their organizational structures traceable to contrasting individualistic versus collectivist behavioral beliefs. The traders from the Islamic world developed in-group social communications networks to enforce collective action which, while effective in relatively small homogeneous ethnic groups, do not lend themselves to the impersonal exchange that arises from the growing size of markets and diverse ethnic traders. In contrast the Genoese developed bilateral enforcement mechanisms which entailed the creation of formal legal and political organizations for monitoring and enforcing agreements—an institutional/organizational path that permitted and led to more complex trade and exchange. Greif suggests the generality of these different belief structures for the Latin and Muslim worlds and then makes the connection between such belief structures in the European scene and the development of the economic institutions and organizations described in section III.

But if we accept that there were different behavioral beliefs in different societies and that they induced different forms of institutions and organizations, what produced the beliefs? In chapter 4 I suggested that the origins probably stemmed from fundamental demographic/resource constraints that became embodied in religions since they were the dominant organized belief structures of the pre-modern world. The vast literature dealing with the effect of religious dogma on economic activity is, however, inconclusive since it is possible to pick out specific aspects of almost any religion that are antithetical to economic growth. Some of these are the Islamic opposition to insurance markets and the Christian opposition to interest payments (Kuran 1986).

The proper focus, however, should not be on specific norms but on the learning process by which a particular belief structure—in this case religion—evolves. To briefly recapitulate, the learning process is a function of the way in which a given belief structure filters the information derived from experiences and the different experiences that confront individuals in different societies at different times. Thus one can argue that the Christian religious framework of the Middle Ages provided a hospitable filter for learning that led to adaptations congenial to economic growth; or alternatively that the specific geographic/economic/institutional context of the medieval western world provided the unique experiences responsible for the resultant adaptations. In fact it was a combination of the two sets of experiences that produced the adaptations in the belief structure that were conducive to economic growth and political/civil freedoms. The belief structure embodied in Christian dogma was, despite some notorious contrary illustrations, amenable to evolving in directions that made it hospitable to economic growth. Both Ernst Benz (1966) and Lynn White (1978) maintain that Christian belief gradually evolved the view that nature should serve mankind and that therefore the universe could and should be controlled for economic purposes. Such an attitude is an essential precondition for technological progress. But it was particularly the unique institutional conditions of parts of medieval/early modern Europe that provided the sort of experiences that served as the catalyst to precipitate such perceptions. From this perspective Weber's protestant ethic is a part of the story of this adaptation but is "downstream" from the originating sources.

V

We are now ready to explore the mystery of the unique evolution of western Europe. There are still gaps in our understanding and puzzles to be resolved. Moreover a complete story would devote more attention to the costs associated with economic growth: there were losers—lots of them along the way—whose conditions deteriorated in the course of the changes described. But overall, the material conditions of human beings and the security of persons and property over a range of civil, political, religious, and economic activities improved.

Putting at the center of inquiry the institutional/organizational structure of the society, we can explore the interplay between economic and political organization in the context of changes wrought by changing perceptions of the participants or by forces external to them. The failures of the most likely candidates, China and Islam, point the direction of our inquiry. Centralized political control limits the options, the alternatives that will be pursued in a context of uncertainty about the long-run consequences of political and economic decisions. The lack of large-scale political and economic order created the essential environment hospitable to economic growth and ultimately human freedoms. In that competitive decentralized environment lots of alternatives were pursued; some worked, as in the Netherlands and England, some failed, as in the cases of Spain and Portugal, and some, as in France, fell between these two extremes. But the key to the story is the variety of the options pursued and the increased likelihood (as compared to a single unified policy) that some would turn out to produce economic growth. Even the relative failures in western Europe played an essential role in European development.

The last point deserves special emphasis. It was the dynamic consequences of the competition among fragmented political bodies that resulted in an especially creative environment. Europe was politically fragmented; but it had both a common belief structure derived from Christendom and information and transportation connections that resulted in scientific, technological, and artistic developments in one part spreading rapidly throughout Europe. To treat the Netherlands and England as success stories in isolation from the stimulus received from the rest of Europe (and to a lesser degree Islam and China) is to miss a vital part of the explanation. Italian city states, Portugal, and Germanic states all fell behind the Netherlands and England; but banking, artistic development, improvements in navigation, and printing were just a few of the obvious contributions that the former states made to European advancement.

With the advantage of hindsight can we be more specific? The lack of large-scale order in Europe in the early medieval period meant that the source of decision making was in the town or in the manorial/feudal hierarchy. This decision making was conditioned by the cultural heritage that shaped the initial perceptions of the participants. Let us begin with the role of the town on the continent of Europe.

The towns in medieval western Europe varied—from the Italian city state, to fortress towns built in response to the threat of external aggression, to local administrative towns; but in all cases a key factor in their evolution was the degree of autonomy from external authority they enjoyed. The relative freedom of European towns from such authority was an initial distinguishing factor as compared to towns elsewhere. As economic opportunities emerged with the relative increase in order and therefore a decline in the transaction costs of trade, the towns were in a position to take advantage of the new opportunities—whether it was the Mediterranean trade of the Venetians and Genoese or the woolen and metal trade of the Low Country towns in northwest Europe. The expansion of commerce led to the growth of a new interest group, commercial interests, alongside the traditional nobility, Crown, and clergy. Towns were able to gain liberties often over the opposition of nobles and clergy. This liberty to come and go, to buy and sell as they saw fit was as essential to economic growth as some security of property. The Protestant Reformation evolving in the context of repression introduced a concern for another liberty—liberty of conscience, the freedom to worship as one chose; and economic liberty, religious freedom, and representative government became intertwined issues. The commercial expansion of the eleventh to the fourteenth centuries produced not only an increase in urban places but also the development of commercial networks linking together the trade of northwest Europe and of the Mediterranean. The organizational framework of fairs, guilds, and law merchant facilitated the use of the bill of exchange and required an institutional framework of political and economic order. Order necessitated both the creation of a framework of rules of the game inside the town and the establishment of rules and their enforcement that permitted exchange across political boundaries.

The political/economic order within Low Country towns has been eloquently described by Henri Pirenne (1963). His story is one of the creation of the institutional infrastructure of democratic order within thriving town economies, which was gradually undermined by guild restrictions and conflict between patrician and lesser citizenry over control of the polity. But for Pirenne "the municipal democracies of the Middle Ages consisted, and could only have consisted, of privileged members. They did not, and could not, know the ideal of a liberty and an equality open to all" (ibid., 168). For Pirenne this democracy was pragmatic and unleavened by intellectual pretensions of democracy and egalitarianism and therefore not like modern democracy. That may be correct; but what Pirenne was describing was an integral part of a process of fundamental change. Political reordering and inevitable internal conflicts are everywhere in history a part of the process of economic expansion—a conflict not only internal to the town and its evolving interest groups but also external in its relationship with princes and rulers. To reiterate an ongoing theme of this chapter, change was overwhelmingly an incremental process, building onto and modifying the pre-existing institutional framework and constrained by the belief

structure that prevailed. It is precisely that process of institutional/orga-
nizational incremental evolution that Pirenne describes in his story of
the way the various political and economic organizations evolved and
interacted with each other. It is not an inevitable triumph of democracy
that is taking place, but a struggle for control of the polity. And a belief
structure that embodied modern sentiments of democracy and egalitarianism was surely not a part of the perceptions of that time, either in
the town or in the countryside.

England evolved along a route to economic growth and freedom different from that of the Continent. Being an island made it less vulnera-
ble to conquest and eliminated the need for a standing army. The belief
structure, as Macfarlane makes clear, was different. The Norman conquest, the exception to British invulnerability to external conquest,
produced a more centralized feudal structure than any on the Continent; but as the Magna Carta attests, the Crown could not overstep
the traditional liberties of the barons who had dictated the charter's
terms or those of towns, foreign merchants, and villeins. England's
political institutions also differed in several important ways from those
of its neighbors on the Continent. The most important was the unity
of its parliament. There was a single parliament for the entire country;
no regional estates as in France, Spain, and the Netherlands. There
was also no division into towns, clergy, and nobility. Maitland pointed
out: "It is a noticeable fact that at a very early time, perhaps from the
beginning, the citizens and burgesses sit together with the knights"
(Maitland 1963, 175). Both on the Continent and in England the
changing status of serf, and free labor, on the manor was not guided
by any change in the perception of their inferior status. Rather, the
gradual evolution of longer leases, reduced obligations, and shift to
copyhold (in the west) reflected a change in the relative scarcity of labor
as a consequence of population decline in the fourteenth century, the
alternative opportunities that the towns provided, and the competition
for labor that resulted.

In combination with the development of markets, towns, and trade
as a consequence of the relative improvement of order and the demographic changes, the fiscal crises of princes are part of the story. Such
crises arose as a consequence of the ubiquitous warfare among competing political units and the growing costs of warfare. They played a key

role in the political/economic changes that occurred. Between 1200 and 1500 the many political units in western Europe went through endless conflicts, alliances, and warfare and gradually evolved into nation states although it was not so much the size of the political unit that was critical for survival as it was the ability to increase tax revenues. It had been customary for the ruler to receive revenue in kind and indeed in some cases to move the court from one part of the country to another to consume the goods and services in kind. With the growth of a money economy as a consequence of the economic expansion of the eleventh to fourteenth centuries, revenues became monetized; then in the four-teenth and fifteenth centuries they declined as a result of the fall in land rents because of declining population.

A year of warfare resulted in as much as a fourfold increase in the costs of government—and warfare was endemic. Declining revenues and increasing fiscal costs posed an ever worsening dilemma for Euro-pean princes. Custom and tradition set limits on the exactions they could obtain from lesser lords, and a king who stepped across the boundary of accepted custom faced the possibility of revolt. The king's vassals were sometimes as powerful as he and in concert were more powerful. Moreover vassals could and did sometimes combine with foreign princes to overthrow the king; therefore increased taxation of vassals could place a Crown in jeopardy.

While the degrees of freedom of princes varied, one option available to them was to grant privileges—property rights—in return for reve-nue. As trade and commerce grew beyond the bounds of the town or manor, merchants found that the private costs of protection could be reduced by a larger coercive authority and were willing to pay princes to provide protection. In order to prevent loss of revenue (from eva-sions) rulers granted rights to alienate land or to allow inheritance, thereby establishing more secure and efficient property rights. Towns were granted trading privileges in return for annual payments; alien merchants were granted legal rights and exemptions from guild restric-tions in return for revenue. Guilds received exclusive rights of monop-oly in return for payments to the Crown.

The ubiquitous competition among the evolving nation states was a deep underlying source of change and equally a constraint on the op-tions available to rulers within states. Competition forced the Crown to trade rights and privileges for revenue, including, most fundamentally, the granting to "representative" bodies—variously Parliament, States General, Cortes—control over tax rates and/or certain privileges in return for revenue. Competition among states also offered constituents alternatives—states to which they might flee or send their moveable wealth, thus constraining the ruler's options.

But at this point the stories diverge. Some representative bodies retained and expanded their status and provided the basis for the growth of representative government; others declined or withered away. It was the evolving bargaining strength of rulers vis-à-vis constituents that was decisive. Three considerations were at stake: the size of the potential gains the constituents could realize by the state taking over protection of property; the closeness of substitutes for the existing ruler—that is, the ability of rivals (both within and outside the political unit) to the existing ruler to take over and provide the same (or more) services; and the structure of the economy which determined the benefits and costs to the state of various kinds of taxation.

In the Low Countries, for example, the productive town economies stood to gain substantially by the political order and protection of property rights provided first by the Burgundians and then by Charles V. The structure of the economy built around export trades provided the means for easy-to-collect taxes on trade but not at a level to adversely affect the comparative advantage of the trades. But the demands of Philip II led to the conviction that the economy would continue to prosper only with independence. The resistance was initiated on the authority of the States General which in 1581 issued the Act of Abjuration of allegiance to Phillip II and claimed sovereignty for the provinces themselves. Eventually the seven northern provinces succeeded in achieving independence; the resulting economic/political structure of Amsterdam and the Netherlands was one not only of efficient economic organization but with many of the basic attributes of political and civil freedoms. The powers of the newly independent country—the United Provinces—resided with each province and a unanimity rule meant that the States General must receive the votes of the deputations from all provinces. Cumbersome as that process was, this political structure survived. The polity not only evolved the elements of political representation and democratic decision rules but supported religious freedom (an equally important source of friction with the Spanish Crown). The de facto policy of the United Provinces was one of toleration in the sphere of religion; it was a policy that encouraged immigration of dissenters from various parts of Europe, many of whom contributed to the growth of the Dutch economy.

In England as on the Continent, traditional feudal revenues were a declining portion of total state revenues. England's external trade provided an increasing share of the revenue, including taxes on wine, general merchandise, and wool cloth; but it was the wool export trade in the thirteenth century that was the backbone of augmented Crown revenue. Eileen Power (1941) describes the exchange between the three groups involved in the wool trade: the wool growers as represented in Parliament, the merchants of the staple, and the Crown. In an agreement the merchants achieved a monopoly of the export trade and a depot in Calais, Parliament received the right to set the tax, and the Crown received the revenue. William Stubbs summarized the exchange as follows: "The admission of the right of parliament to legislate, to inquire into abuses, and to share in the guidance of national policy, was practically purchased by the money granted to Edward I and Edward III" (Stubbs 1896, vol. 3, 599).

With the Tudors the English Crown was at the zenith of its powers, but it never sought the unilateral control over taxing power that the crowns of France and Spain achieved. The confiscation of monastery lands and possessions by Henry VIII alienated many peers and much of the clergy and as a consequence "Henry had need of the House of Commons and he cultivated it with sedulous care" (Elton 1953, 4). The Stuarts inherited what the Tudors had sown and the evolving controversy between the Crown and Parliament is a well-known tale. Two aspects of this controversy are noteworthy for this analysis. One was the evolving perception of the common law as the supreme law of the land—a position notably championed by Sir Edward Coke—and the other was the connection made between monopoly and a denial of liberty as embodied in the Crown grants of monopoly privileges. As David Sacks put it: "The concept of liberty grew in antithesis to the growth of a theory of state power which had its concrete expression in the creation of economic monopolies. The focus on the grievance of monopolies helped sustain a powerful intellectual connection between the protection of individual rights and the preservation of the commonweal" (Sacks 1992, 86).

The Spanish Crown, in contrast, evolved into an absolutist monarchy. The nation state that emerged under Ferdinand and Isabella joined two very different regions, Aragon and Castile. The former, comprising Valencia, Aragon, and Cataloni, had been reconquered from the Arabs in the last half of the thirteenth century and had become a major commercial center. Its Cortes reflected the interest of merchants and played a significant role in public affairs. Indeed, had Aragon determined the future of Spain its history would have been very different. Castile, which had been continually engaged in warfare against Moors and in internal strife, had no such heritage of strong merchant groups. Its Cortes was relatively less effective and Isabella succeeded in gaining control of unruly barons and of church policy as well. A centralized monarchy and resultant bureaucracy ensued; and it was Castile that determined the institutional evolution of Spain (and ultimately of Latin America, as well).

The era of Spanish hegemony was made possible by the income from the Habsburg empire and the new world treasure, but as revenue from those sources declined the Crown of necessity turned to the desperate expedients of taxation and confiscation briefly described in the preceding paragraphs—with disastrous results. Economic monopolies and centralized political controls went hand in hand. The path that Spain was traveling proved durable and led to three centuries of economic stagnation and political instability which only ended with the demise of Franco in the mid-twentieth century. Moreover the Spanish heritage carried over into the new world of Latin America a set of institutions and organizations that produced neither sustained economic growth nor sustained political and civil freedoms.

The divergent evolution of the Netherlands and England, on the one hand, and Spain—and France—on the other can be immediately attributed to the different bargaining strength of constituents and rulers and the three underlying sources of that bargaining strength: the gains to constituent groups of the state taking over protection of property; the closeness of substitutes for the existing ruler; the economic structure which determined the yields to various taxes. In turn we can trace the particular geographic/economic/institutional pattern that produced the divergent conditions. Bargaining strength may be the immediate source of change but it is incomplete, and it would be misleading to ignore the complementary role played by the belief structure. Western Europe had the initial common belief structure of Latin Christendom. But that initial belief structure evolved differently in different parts of Europe as a consequence of diverse experiences. In the Netherlands and England the experiences fostered the evolution of the belief structure in directions that led to modern perceptions of freedom. In contrast, Spanish experiences perpetuated not only an aversion to economic activity but also beliefs underlying the medieval hierarchical order.

The evolution of the belief structure in England is most succinctly captured by J. H. Hexter's contrast of the medieval liberties of England in 1500—"a changing body of particular claims under the protection of law for those who had them"—with the Petition of Right enacted by Parliament in 1628—a Petition which concerns "itself with freedom at the level of its foundations"—the enactment of which, Hexter (1992, 1 and 2) contended, "is the decisive first step in the direction of modern freedom, of liberty as we know it in our world." Access to medieval liberties was determined by the hierarchical structure of the society; bondsmen—slaves, villeins, serfs, and other dependent individuals—were excluded from access. The Petition of Right, in contrast, established for all Englishmen a set of rights protected by law—a law enacted by Parliament. The changing perceptions about the rights of individuals, from the medieval views of status to the seventeenth-century view of Englishmen as freeborn, reflected the evolution of the belief structure between 1500 and 1628. The positive combination of the belief structure with the particular conditions that existed in the Netherlands and England led to the institutional evolution of the economy and polity. This combination fostered the intellectual changes that produced not just the Protestant Reformation but an evolving belief structure that induced behavior conducive both to economic growth and to the evolution of freedoms. The contrasting circumstances in Spain and to a lesser degree France shaped the evolution of the belief structure in ways that reinforced the existing institutional structure and stifled both economic growth and political/civil freedoms.

The Rise and Fall of the Soviet Union

THE RISE of the Western world was, in effect, a success story in which the sequential evolution of beliefs modified by experiences gradually resulted in the changes producing modern economic growth. It was a trial and error process interlaced with good luck. But if we seek to understand the process of change as an exercise in the intentionality of the players, there is no better case in all of history than the rise and fall of the Soviet Union.[1] It exemplifies

1. the ongoing relationship between beliefs, the way they are formed, and how experience modifies a given belief structure;

2. the role of the structure of political decision making in determining whose beliefs get implemented;

3. the "institutionalization" of beliefs via the formal rule-making structure;

4. the feedback on the consequences of the specific institutional policies; and

5. the factors that determine the effectiveness of that feedback in modifying policies in the face of unanticipated or undesired consequences.

This chapter does not attempt a detailed account of the complex evolution of the Soviet Union. Its more modest objective is to highlight this story by looking at the beginning and end of the Soviet Union. The beginning brings out all of the complexities in the deliberate creation of an entirely new form of societal organization and the difficulties of such an endeavor; the end illustrates the problems of making fundamental changes in a society with all of the built in "rigidities" that were a conse-

---

[1] I am no expert on the Soviet Union and have leaned heavily on those who are. Without in any way implicating them in my account I would like to express my thanks to Gregory Grossman, Michael McFaul, John Litwack, Andre Schleifer, and Peter Boetke.

quence of the way that society was put together. More than anything else this story highlights the wide gap between intentions and outcomes and the fragility of societal order in the process of fundamental economic, political, and social change. Despite enormous accomplishments—repulsing the Nazi invasion, the achievement of super power status, immense technological development, and perhaps most impressive of all, the conversion of a poorly educated populace to one endowed with immense human capital—the Soviet Union simply fell apart.

I

The common view of Marxists immediately after the Revolution was that tools of political economy were useful only in a capitalist economy and therefore all the basic categories of political economy such as commodity, value, price, profit, wages, should be done away with—it was necessary to start all over again. Markets and money should disappear. The sequence of events from war communism through the New Economic Policy to the first five year plan in 1928 reflected the evolving views of Lenin, Stalin, Trotsky, Bukharin, and others. Initial "theory" was being molded and modified by learning—learning derived from revised beliefs in the context of the changing external environment.

What was the initial theory and how did external events modify it? Certainly the era of war communism appears to have had a pragmatic set of policies responding to endless immediate crises. To begin with almost everything was nationalized including land, wages were to be paid in kind rather than in monetary units, production decisions were to be made in physical units, and compulsory assignment of workers was designed to break away from a capitalist mode of production. The negative incentives with respect to worker productivity and peasant agricultural output had the expected consequences. Decision making was in the hands of the Bolshevik elite, the "vanguard of the working class," who concentrated on policy making yet whose ever enlarging bureaucracy required delegation and led to the Party developing elaborate controls over the bureaucracy.[2]

---

[2] I have not treated in this brief chapter the evolution of political control. For a discussion, see Roeder (1993).

Marx and Engels had envisioned a dialectical movement from feudalism to capitalism to socialism and therefore it was necessary to achieve full-blown capitalism before socialism could develop. "But Marx and Engels had another prediction, specifically addressed to Russia of the early 1880s. According to them, a revolution in Russia could occur and trigger a proletarian revolution in the West, but the two would have to complement each other for a socialist orientation (based on the Russian land commune) of the Russian revolution to become possible. In other words, the unique, but still primitive, Russian conditions would not carry a socialist revolution on their own" (Lewin 1995, 152).

As time went on it became clear that world revolution was not in the cards and Russia would have to build socialism on its own. But that still left open the question of the degree to which the road to socialism had to pass through capitalism. Was the creation of the NEP a deliberate strategy or was it a pragmatic response to the desperate need to get more output from peasant agriculture? "But from the latter part of 1921 [Bukharin] came to see it as, first, a necessary retreat, and second, from 1922, the preliminary for a renewed advance upon the forces of capital. In this he was following Lenin, who from 1922 began proclaiming that the retreat was over, and that, just as the Japanese had failed to take Port Arthur by direct assault in 1905 only to succeed by a long siege, so the Bolsheviks had failed to establish socialism in the Soviet Union by direct assault but would do so by the 'siege' tactics of NEP" (Ferdinand 1992).

Throughout the 1920s the tradeoff between investment in agriculture and investment in industrial expansion was an ongoing controversy. Those who advocated concentrating on agriculture first felt that the immediate results would provide for the rapid expansion that could then permit investment in heavy industry with its much longer period of gestation. Trotsky, in contrast, adopted the views of the leading theoretician of the left, E. Preobrazhensky, that heavy industry should have priority with emphasis on expanding industrial capacity.

Investment in industry was growing by 1926 but there was a continuing shortage of industrial goods and continuing crises in agricultural procurement; the grain crisis of 1927–28 precipitated a search for new policies to deal with the peasantry. Thus severe price controls on farm prices (especially grain) led to a drop in market deliveries, which in turn increased the pressure for the universal collectivization of private agriculture. "It was the unplanned character of the whole process that forced on the state ever more 'planning' meaning simply the need to enlarge the scope of administrative controls, and the takeover of the whole national economy by state apparatus. The more bottlenecks and crisis areas that appeared, the greater the urge to close loopholes by putting the hands on more levers. In other words, this is the process through which a fully nationalized 'command economy' emerged—in a short space of time—with internal mechanisms pushing to a very centralized pyramid shaped power structure" (Lewin 1995, 101–2).

This account of the early years should not be surprising in the light of the basic arguments of this study. An initial belief system was forced by the ongoing crises of revolution, civil war, and starvation to ad-hoc responses to each new crisis, reflecting as the beliefs did the very imperfect and primitive understanding that the players had of the fundamental structure of an operating economy and their even more primitive understanding of the necessary incentive structure to accomplish their objectives. Complicating the story was the emerging and ongoing struggle for power between the players, settled by Stalin's victory and his imposition of the first five year plan with its collectivization of agriculture and investment in heavy industry. Accompanying this imposition was development of a gigantic state apparatus designed to plan all the vital functions of the society.

The underlying rationale for the evolving plan of industrial development was a deep and abiding belief in the supremacy of engineers as the key players in the planning process—a view supported by the technocracy movement of the 1920s which was known to the leading Bolsheviks (cf. Lenin's famous slogan "Communism=Soviet Power plus the Electrification of the Whole Country").[3]

II

The Soviet regime consolidated by Stalin was one of the strongest states of the twentieth century. Under Stalin, the Soviet state set the creation of socialism (in one country) as its primary objective and then used coercion,

[3] I am indebted to Gregory Grossman for calling my attention to technocracy as well as for many other helpful insights.

violence, and mass murder to accomplish the task. Stalin's USSR was the paradigmatic totalitarian state.... This state no longer existed in August 1991. While still totalitarian in structure, the Soviet state had atrophied and weakened considerably throughout the Brezhnev years. Gorbachev's reforms further weakened the capacity of the state to define and implement policy goals. Under Gorbachev the main administrative agent of the Soviet system, the communist party of the Soviet Union (CPSU) lost its "leading role." No new institution emerged to fill the void. (McFaul 1995, 224)

Can we fill in the details of this extraordinary decline between 1985 and 1991?

The place to begin is with the prescient comment of George Kennan made in 1947: "If... anything is ever to occur to disrupt the unity and efficacy of the Party as a political instrument, Soviet Russia might be changed overnight from one of the strongest to one of the weakest and most pitiable of national societies."[4] In fact it was precisely this phenomenon—the destruction of the party as a political instrument—that appears to have been the immediate cause of demise. But first we must step back to provide the historical background to the collapse in the years between 1985 and 1991.

There were relatively few organizational changes in Stalin's last two years. Major changes had to wait until after the death of the great dictator. On 5 March 1953 his henchmen found themselves successors to his heritage, a great country, the second military and industrial power, yet one with many weaknesses, unevenly developed. Great scientific achievements had been made but the housing situation was still appalling, consumers' goods of poor quality, the villages primitive. Even within a single sector, grain cultivation for instance, large modern combine-harvesters were used alongside totally unmechanized hand operations in the process of cleaning, drying, loading. What was to be done about over centralization, lack of acceptable (or accepted) investment criteria, agricultural prices, the deficiency of the trading network, the breakdown in material supplies? How could it be tolerated that a country capable of making an A-bomb could not supply its citizens with eggs? How could necessary initiative be encouraged under conditions of terror? (Nove 1969, 314)

[4] As quoted in Grossman (1998, 24).

After Stalin's death the cardinal problem for the Soviet economy became reform. Major reforms—those that would substantially reduce the role of central planning and hierarchical *administration*; direct production targets, price and wage controls; and correspondingly increase the role of markets, of decentralized decision making, and of functional non-state ownership—were never undertaken. Minor reforms which retained the existing set of institutions but aimed to improve their efficiency were tried as a result of a growing perception of serious problems of an across-the-board nature and after long-term covert or even overt discussion.[5]

During the Brezhnev era it was apparent that the rate of growth had declined but reform efforts came to naught in the context of an entrenched and powerful bureaucracy that had evolved as a part of the monolithic Soviet state. Gregory Grossman, after listing a number of proximate sources of decline, goes on to say, "a succession of inept, partial, repeatedly failing economic reforms eroded confidence in the future of the traditional system, accelerating the fall as it began to sway" (1998, 26). To the traditional causes of illicit wealth in private hands, ubiquitous corruption, an explosion of violent organized crime, and a reorientation of bureaucratic loyalties, he adds, and stresses, the rapid rise of the shadow economy.

When Gorbachev came to power he sought to revitalize the economy through liberalization of economic and political institutions. "Only after three years of attempting to introduce economic reform through the existing set of political institutions did Gorbachev conclude that he could not rely on the existing nexus of party and state institutions to implement his reform agenda. He reasoned that he could only proceed with perestroika (reorganization) by changing the institutions of governance as a way both to undermine his opponents empowered within the existing institutional arrangement and to strengthen new proponents of reform in society" (McFaul 1999). The result was the rapid disintegration of the existing control system.

Perestroika was never a clearly thought out reform program. At the plenary meeting of the Central Committee of the Communist Party of

---

[5] These comments summarize comments made to me in a letter by Gregory Grossman (no date) dealing with efforts at post-Stalin reform.

the Soviet Union (CPSU) in June 1987 a set of reforms gave directors increasing autonomy in setting wages, prices, and output targets. The next year the Law on Cooperatives legalized private economic activity. Both reforms gave directors increased incentives to hide production, divert resources for personal use, and skim profits (McFaul 2001, 42).

> Directors, as knowledgeable agents for different principals, began to acquire de-facto property rights over their entities. First they assumed rights to consumption. Because the principal could not monitor all production at the enterprise level, directors had opportunities for personal consumption and exploitation of resources and could also control consumption by other enterprise employees.
>
> Second, directors made profits. By hiding revenue or skimming extra production, directors supplemented their personal wealth at the expense of the principal. An extensive black market offered irresistible opportunities; and there was no market inhibitors to shirking. Moreover, under Gorbachev a series of reforms allowed small enterprises and cooperatives further enhancing the directors' opportunities to derive profits from state assets. In accordance with these new laws, entrepreneurial directors set up parasitic cooperatives, collectively owned entities, lease agreements, and joint ventures, which became profit centers feeding off the assets of large state enterprises. All profitable transactions with outside contractors, and especially foreign contractors, were channeled through these small enterprises, leaving profits offshore with little or no benefit to the state enterprise as a whole. Directors thus reaped profits from property without bearing the risks or liabilities associated with total ownership. Directors of Soviet enterprises never acquired the third right—the right to transfer property or the right of alienation. But then in the socialist economy, only the principal (the state) could exercise this right. The system, that is, had only one de jure owner, making transfers within the Soviet Union meaningless. (McFaul 1995, 222–23)

Perestroika also served to unhinge the political structure that had provided stability within the Soviet political system—a structure based on informal institutions that "signaled to Party leaders and economic managers at all levels their privileges and responsibilities as the governing class in the USSR" (McFaul 2001, 43). These privileges and responsibilities were threatened by the economic changes that gave enterprise directors greater autonomy and thus decreased the power of party bureaucrats. Resistance within the party led Gorbachev to purge party leaders as the enemies of reform and alter some of the rules governing internal party politics (McFaul 2001, 45). Glasnost, or openness, was aimed at creating greater freedom of expression in order to undermine the stranglehold of party leaders. The reduction of censorship and the relaxing of laws limiting freedom of speech, the return from exile of Andrei Sakharov, and allowing competitive nomination for delegates to the nineteenth Party Conference (1988) all contributed to undermining the party bureaucracy.

Glasnost succeeded. The 1989 election led to an explosion of political activity, media criticism, and an array of political movements.

> Initially, these forces from below were Gorbachev's allies against the conservative midlevel bureaucracy of the Communist party. Quickly, however, the kind, extent, and pace of change demanded from below overtook Gorbachev's own reform agenda. Beginning first with the International Group of Deputies in the USSR Congress, political actors bent on truly revolutionary change began to organize against the traditional ruling institutions of the Soviet Regime. Led by Boris Yeltsin, this new political force rapidly gravitated toward the "organization of counterhegemony": collective projects for an alternative future. While initially vague, several antisystemic themes eventually crystallized to help situate these challengers in diametric opposition to Gorbachev's ancien regime. (McFaul 1999, 114)

Chapter 8 explored the delicate balance between order and disorder in societies; the account of the Soviet Union suggests just how delicate order is when the underlying political structure is eroded. Steven Solnick succinctly summarizes the process as follows:

> When officials at the top of organizations proved unable to control the activities of their subordinates, they invite doubts about what resources they still controlled. These doubts spread the erosion of authority within the organizational structure, as local officials who were still loyal began to wonder whether their subservience might leave them completely disenfranchised if the center collapsed. Ill-fated attempts to reassert central control— for example in the Balkan states—only exacerbated the crisis by offering further proof of the center's weakness.

Ultimately, at precisely the juncture where the effectiveness of policy reform depended on a coherent institutional response, local officials defected en mass and the pillars of the Soviet System crumbled. In effect, Soviet institutions were victimized by the organizational equivalent of a colossal "bank run" in which local officials rushed to claim their assets before the bureaucratic doors shut for good. As in a bank run, the loss of confidence in the institutions makes its demise a self-fulfilling prophecy. Unlike a bank run, the defecting officials were not depositors claiming their rightful assets, but employees of the state appropriating state assets.

From this perspective, the image of a "disintegrating" state can be seen as seriously incomplete. Soviet institutions did not simply atrophy or dissolve but were actively pulled apart by officials at all levels seeking to extract assets that were in any way fungible. Where organizational assets were more specific to their particular use by the state, as in the case of draft boards, for example, hierarchical structures proved more resilient. Where organizational assets were chiefly cash and buildings, hierarchical breakdown was almost total. At both ends of the spectrum, the catalysts of state collapse were the agents of the state itself. Once the bank run was on, these officials were not merely stealing resources from the state, they were stealing the state itself. (Solnick 1998, 7)

While the details of the demise of the Soviet Union are the subject of an enormous literature and controversy, the underlying explanation is not complicated viewed from the perspective of the institutional analysis that forms the core of this study. Adaptive efficiency entails an institutional structure that in the face of the ubiquitous uncertainties of a non-ergodic world will flexibly try various alternatives to deal with novel problems that continue to emerge over time. In turn this institutional structure entails a belief structure that will encourage and permit experimentation and equally will wipe out failures. The Soviet Union represented the very antithesis of such an approach.

Improving Economic Performance

THE PROBLEMS of achieving sustained economic growth should be apparent from the preceding chapters. The economic history of the past half century is littered with the debris of economies that failed to develop, from sub-Saharan African economies to the former republics of the Soviet Union. Yes, the economies of the world have generally achieved significant economic growth. A survey of the world economies at the beginning of the twenty-first century reveals unprecedented prosperity as compared to economic conditions in the past. Yet more than a billion people around the earth still exist on less than one dollar a day and more than two-and-a-half billion on less than two dollars a day; stop-and-go growth still characterizes most of Latin America; Japan has been mired in stagnation; Indonesia is in a precarious position vis-à-vis surviving as an entity. On the face of it this is puzzling. We not only know the conditions underlying successful economic growth—the new growth economics spells them out—but we even know the kind of institutions necessary to undergird successful economic growth. Moreover the stock of "useful" knowledge—the underlying determinant of the potential for economic growth—continues to develop at an undiminished pace.

The previous chapters have attempted to make the problem clear. If economic growth simply was a function of the growth in the stock of knowledge and technology then the future well-being of the human race would appear to be assured. Once we take into account the complex, and still far from understood, interaction between consciousness and evolving cultures no such assurance exists. The way in which beliefs → institutions → organizations → policies → outcomes evolves has led to unparalleled economic well-being and to endless disasters and human misery. We still have some distance to go before we understand completely the process of economic growth but we have learned a good deal. The previous chapters have explored three key dilemmas in the process of economic *change*—the movement from personal to impersonal exchange, the complex interdependent, institutional structure that characterizes the modern human environment, and a non-ergodic world. It will be useful to confront explicitly the sources of these dilemmas so that we can understand better how to deal with them. We begin with beliefs and the consequent institutional structure and then explore the problems arising from the evolving structure of polities and economies and resultant transaction costs as well as the problems arising from distributed knowledge. We can then make concrete suggestions for improving performance.

I

Even the most cursory survey of the existing beliefs around the world does not offer an optimistic view consistent with the underlying implicit notions of the rationality assumption. Religious fundamentalism, ethnic hatreds, racist stereotypes, superstitions, all shape choices with monotonous persistence. In a Coasian world the players would always choose that policy that maximized aggregate well-being with compensation for any losers; but the real transaction costs are frequently prohibitive reflecting deep-seated beliefs and prejudices that translate into such prohibitive transaction costs. It is more than two hundred years since Adam Smith explained the underlying sources of the wealth of nations but the extent to which such views are embedded in the decision-making process of those shaping political/economic change is problematic.

We have now come to understand enough about institutions to be able to pinpoint the sources of poor performance. They have their origins in path dependence. We inherit the artifactual structure—the institutions, beliefs, tools, techniques, external symbol storage systems—from the past. Broadly speaking this is our cultural heritage and we ignore it in decision making at our peril—the peril of failing in our attempt to improve economic performance. The degree to which such cultural heritage is "malleable" via deliberate modification is still very imperfectly understood. At any time it imposes severe constraints on the ability to effectuate change. Let me just enumerate the resultant problems:

1. The institutional structure inherited from the past may reflect a set of beliefs that are impervious to change either because the proposed changes run counter to that belief system or because the proposed alteration in institutions threatens the leaders and entrepreneurs of existing organizations. Where fundamentally competing beliefs exist side by side, the problems of creating a viable set of institutional arrangements are increased and may make the establishment of consensual political rules a prescription for short-run disaster.

2. The artifactual structure that defines the performance of an economy comprises interdependent institutions; changing just one institution in an attempt to get the desired performance is always an incomplete and sometimes a counter-productive activity.

3. A mixture of formal institutions, informal institutions, and their enforcement characteristics defines institutional performance; and while the formal institutions may be altered by fiat, the informal institutions are not amenable to deliberate short-run change and the enforcement characteristics are only very imperfectly subject to deliberate control.

If we had perfect feedback on the consequences of our institutional policies then we could correctly understand whether our actions achieved the desired objectives. However, there is so much "noise" in the system that even if we desire to understand the results we might not be able to have clear signals; and the principal/agent problems in the hierarchical chain of information that produces feedback may militate against getting a correct appraisal. Altering the performance of an economy for the better takes time—a lot longer than the time horizon of the politician who must approve such changes. In the short run the reform may necessitate alterations that leave some of the players worse off, and if they have access to the political process they may very well derail the reform.

II

It is easy to describe the ideal political model—both the authoritarian version and the consensual version have been briefly described in the preceding chapters. The four "ideal" components can be restated as follows:

1. an institutional matrix that produces a set of organizations and establishes a set of rights and privileges;

2. a stable structure of exchange relationships in both political and economic markets;

3. an underlying structure that credibly commits the state to a set of political rules and enforcement that protects organizations and exchange relationships;

4. conformity as a result of some mixture of norm internalization and coercive enforcement.

The ideal economic model comprises a set of economic institutions that provide incentives for individuals and organizations to engage in productive activity. But such a general formulation does not take us very far. The creation of a set of property rights that will lead to an effective price system is a necessary step, but again the substance is in the details. With transaction costs defined as the costs of measuring what is being exchanged and of enforcing agreements we must devise a property rights system that provides low cost transacting in the production and exchange of goods and services. Because each factor and product market has different physical, technical, informational, and political characteristics the creation of the general conditions of a price system must be supplemented by structuring each market with the necessary institutional framework to produce "efficient" results. Moreover since the above characteristics will change over time it is essential that such structures be modified over time.

We need to explore in much more detail the sources of transaction costs in an economy. There are transaction costs in

1. measuring the multiple valuable dimensions of a good or service;
2. the protection of individual property rights;
3. the integration of the dispersed knowledge of a society;
4. the enforcement of agreements.

We will look at each in turn.

1. Goods and services typically have multiple dimensions that have utility to the individual. To the degree that these individual dimensions can be measured we can define property rights more precisely and thereby increase the utility to the individual and reduce the costs of exchange.

2. The development of effective third party enforcement with all that it entails in terms of institutions and organizations is always supplemented by resources the individual devotes to protection of his/her property.

3. The greater the specialization and division of labor in a society the more dispersed is the knowledge in a society and the more resources must be devoted to integrating that dispersed knowledge.

4. Enforcement of agreements involves the costs of monitoring and metering exchanges to see that the terms of exchange are being lived up to and developing effective punishment for violations.

Improving economic performance means lowering production and transaction costs and the key is modifying institutions to accomplish this objective. We can do so by

1. the development of a uniform system of weights and measures, technological research for better measurement, and improved specification of property rights;

2. the creation of an effective judicial system to reduce the costs of contract enforcement;

3. the development of institutions to integrate the dispersed knowledge in a society as well as to monitor and meter agreements and adjudicate disputes.

It should be emphasized that the institutions that have emerged in the Western world, such as property rights and judicial systems, do not have to be faithfully copied in developing countries. The key is the incentive structure that is created, not the slavish imitation of western institutions. Starting with the household responsibility system, the Chinese developed an incentive structure which managed to produce rapid economic development without any of the standard recipes of the West. However, down the road the Chinese must embed the incentive system in the political/economic structure if they are to continue their rapid development and that will probably require institutions that come much closer to having the adaptively efficient features of western societies.

III

Poorly performing economies have an institutional matrix that does not provide incentives for productivity-improving activities. The explanation is twofold. One, their existing institutional structure has created organizations with a vested interest in the existing structure. Two, dispersed knowledge requires a complex mixture of institutions and organizations to create effective product and factor markets and we do not completely understand the proper mixture for achieving results. The most common source of the former problem is the persistence of "clientelism," the consequences of attempting to extend personal exchange into larger economic and political markets. While such extensions in economic markets may produce, and indeed have produced substantial enlargements of economic markets, in political markets they typically produce poorly performing democracies characterized by monopoly, corruption, targeted spending, and overall poor economic as well as political performance.[1]

The dismal history of modern sub-Saharan Africa is a telling indictment of our inadequate knowledge of the politics of economic development; the political history of Latin America is only slightly less depressing; and the experience of Russia in the last ten years of the twentieth century is a compelling lesson in our poor understanding of the creation of an effective polity. Overcoming the entrenched interests perpetuating the status quo is one problem, the complex relationship between formal rules and informal constraints another.

The radical decline worldwide in information costs together with the obvious material success of the high income countries has provided an important impetus for change. Windows of opportunity for changes in the formal rules occur when the organizations supporting the status quo have been weakened by poor performance, exposure of corruption, or radical reduction in information about better performance elsewhere. Moreover the formal rules specifying the four components of an ideal political model can be at least superficially enacted. But making such formal rules effective requires both complementary informal constraints and enforcement. There is a good deal of argument and contradictory evidence on just how long it takes for the development of such informal norms. Certainly essential to the successful long-run performance of the developed economies have been deeply entrenched informal norms that limit the degrees of freedom of the political players.

---

[1] For a discussion of the effect of clientelism on democracy see Philip Keefer (2002).

And enforcement entails both the creation of the necessary institutions and organizations and the complementary informal constraints. An authoritarian ruler dedicated to promoting economic growth has a substantial advantage in the short run. In effect he/she can establish the four conditions set out above for an effective polity. But in the longer run a consensual polity is essential since the persistence of the ruler's dedication to the conditions making for good economic performance will ultimately be undermined by crises or mortality.

The creation of a stable consensual polity takes time and simply putting in place the formal rules is a recipe for disappointment, not to say disaster. As mentioned earlier most Latin American countries after independence adopted their constitution from that of the United States but with radically different consequences. Successful consensual polities require a deep underlying set of norms to constrain the players and developing these takes time. An incremental process of increasing indigenous skills, in which external aid in the form of providing educational, medical, or other assistance will explicitly be concerned with transferring those skills to the developing country, will gradually build up the human capital that is a necessary prerequisite for a consensual polity. Obviously any deliberate effort to broaden the human capital of poorly performing economies must be built on an explicit understanding of the cultural heritage of that economy.

IV

The complex interdependent structure of our modern political economies has evolved its modern form over time and usually without deliberate planning. As a result we have very imperfect understanding of the structure essential to their performance. But as soon as we attempt to improve the performance of poorly performing economies we become very conscious of what complex problems result from this interdependence. The integration of the dispersed knowledge requires more than a price system for its accomplishment. As noted in chapter 9 modern specialization introduces a specific kind of transaction cost—that of ascertaining the measurement and performance characteristics of goods and services which are alien to one's specialized knowledge but are a necessary requirement in order to be able to combine dispersed knowledge effectively.

Adam Smith's wealth of nations was a function of specialization and division of labor. But the logic of specialization and division of labor implies a world in which individuals know a great deal about their specialty but in consequence know less about the rest of their world. Hayek emphasized the crucial additional point that in consequence individuals can have only a very imperfect understanding of the overall character of the political/economic system. Hayek was certainly correct that our knowledge is always fragmentary at best and his pioneering study in cognitive science provided the foundation for accounting for our imperfect understanding. But Hayek failed to understand that we have no choice but to undertake social engineering even though we may certainly agree with his winning argument with socialist planners about the efficacy of a price system over alternatives. We must return to the nature of consciousness to put the overall argument in proper perspective. Consciousness is about human intentionality—an intentionality built upon the extraordinary imaginative and creative mind that humans have evolved. But as noted earlier, consciousness is the source both of our creative being and of our capacity for self-destruction.

The essence of understanding the role of institutions in a society is to recognize that they embody the intentionality of our conscious mind. The structure, whether of individual markets or an entire political/economic system, is a human-made creation whose functioning is neither automatic nor "natural." Moreover the structure must be continually altered with changes in the basic parameters of technology, information, and human capital if it is to function well (however defined). In the absence of externalities, imperfect and asymmetric information, and free riding we can envision a price system confronting the economic complexities of change. But such a vision leaves out human beings with the still incompletely understood features of human behavior in a non-ergodic world. These features include the way humans interpret their evolving world, particularly with respect to the interplay between economic changes and changes in the polity but equally with respect to alterations in military technology which destabilize an existing equilibrium between the parts of the society. As noted in chapter

2, in an ergodic world we would eventually get it right, but in the world of continual novel change that we live in no such guarantee exists. The best recipe for confronting such novel situations is the one that Hayek put forth many years ago and that has been the source of U.S. material success, which is the maintenance of institutions that permit trial and error experiments to occur. Such a structure entails not only a variety of institutions and organizations so that alternative policies can be tried but also effective means of eliminating unsuccessful solutions. Adaptive efficiency evolves only after a relatively long period of evolving informal norms and we know of no shortcut to this process.

V

With all these caveats to our understanding of creating improved economic performance let us see if we can be more positive about the subject.

1. The first requirement for improving economic performance is to have a clear understanding of the sources of poor economic performance. Measuring the cost of transacting in various factor and product markets is an essential first step. With that information we can trace back the sources of poor performance to their origins in the institutional/organizational structure. But high transaction costs will frequently have militated against any production at all of some goods and services that given the factor endowments should be profitable investments. Therefore an essential additional requirement is an intimate understanding of the potential prospects of the economy so that with a reduction in transaction costs one could envision an expansion in the variety of goods and services that the economy would produce.

2. In order to improve the institutional structure we must first have a clear understanding of the sources of that institutional framework. We must know where we have been in order to know where we can be going. Understanding the cultural heritage of a society is a necessary condition for making "doable" change. We must have not only a clear understanding of the belief structure underlying the existing institutions but also margins at which the belief system may be amenable to changes that will make possible the implementation of more productive

institutions. Only then will we have a knowledge of the sources of the existing institutions, their organizational underpinnings, and insights into possible structural reform.

3. In the face of competition from already developed economies, underdeveloped economies face the additional problems involved in integrating the dispersed knowledge essential to low cost performance. The "global economy" is not a level playing field. The already developed economies have a major advantage in the institutional/organizational framework that (however imperfectly) captures the productivity potential inherent in integrating the dispersed knowledge essential to efficient production in a world of specialization. One cannot create that institutional/organizational matrix over night. Therefore a variety of governmental interventions—with all the caveats necessary for their termination over time—may be essential in the short run to be competitive.

4. A viable polity that will put in place the necessary economic institutions and provide effective enforcement is a necessary prerequisite for improved performance. In a country without a heritage of formal and informal consensual political institutions, the road to an effective political system requires either an authoritarian ruler with an understanding, desire, and ability to put in place the necessary economic rules and enforce them, or the much more lengthy process of piece meal development through non-governmental organizations (NGOs) and effective foreign aid in which educational, health, judicial, or other assistance is effectively designed and delivered with the objective of transferring the essential knowledge and skills to the resident population.[2] An externality by-product will be a gradual accumulation of the necessary political human capital to build an effective consensual polity. I know of no effective shortcut to this alternative and it entails the additional requirement that the existing government be "induced" not to intervene in preventing such local improvements and transfers of knowledge.

Where the essential conditions for a consensual polity exist, the development of institutional rules that provide for greater transparency in the polity will enable more effective monitoring of the polity. There is an immense literature on effective (that is, conducive to promoting

---

[2] Mwabu, et al. (2001) discuss some of the issues involved in such provision.

economic growth) political policy, all variants to one degree or another of Madison's insights in the *Federalist Papers.*

As noted above, alteration of the economic rules entails winners and losers and it is essential to be aware of them, of their access to the political process and therefore of the ability of losers to negate the proposed alterations. While "Coasian" solutions are not always possible, awareness of the costs and benefits can result in institutional alterations that can mitigate opposition.

The foregoing pages should make it abundantly clear that there is no set formula for achieving economic development. No economic model can capture the intricacies of economic growth in a particular society. While the sources of productivity growth are well known, the process of economic growth is going to vary with every society, reflecting the diverse cultural heritages and the equally diverse geographic, physical, and economic settings. The message of this book is that you have to understand the process of economic growth before you can improve performance and then you must have an intimate understanding of the individual characteristics of that society before you are ready to try to change it. Then you must have an understanding of the intricacies of institutional change to be effective in undertaking that change.

Where Are We Going?

THE UNPRECEDENTED economic development of the past several centuries with its consequences for material progress and life expectancy has, not surprisingly, provided a context and perspective to humans of continuous progress; and with good reason. The growth in the stock of knowledge has produced material improvements beyond the wildest dreams of our ancestors. The current definition of poverty in the United States (approximately $18,000 a year for a family of four) would have exceeded (given appropriate deflators) the living standard of all but a miniscule fraction of humans several centuries ago. As already mentioned, the criterion of progress is sometimes confined to growth in the stock of knowledge; and there do not appear to be diminishing returns setting in to that growth as applied to solving problems of scarcity. But a focus of this study is on institutions and the way humans have developed them to deal with uncertainty. And here too we have managed to create complex societies composed of institutions that apply the stock of knowledge to produce productive economies. Yet when we explore the human condition in this larger context of the overall political/economic/social structure, the results are ambiguous.

The argument of this book has implications for the way we perceive the future of human beings. We have only limited vision to see into the future and the implications for the future prospects of humans are clearly uncertain. Understanding the process of economic change entails comprehending the enormous improvements in economic well-being as well as coming to grips with the deep uncertainties that have characterized that evolution and confront us in the future. In this final chapter I very briefly consider some of the implications of this approach for the future of the human condition. In succession I explore the evolution of beliefs, novelty and the adaptability of humans, the uncertain success of institutional adaptation, and the limits to adaptive efficiency.

I

It should be clear from the foregoing chapters that not only is our understanding of ourselves very imperfect but the very nature of consciousness is a double-edged sword. Consciousness both is the source and inspiration for the wonders of human creativity and all that that implies about the positive aspects of the human condition, and equally is the source of the superstitions, dogmas, and religions that (together with the accompanying cultural conditioning) produced the Holocaust, endless wars, human savagery, and modern (and non-modern) terrorism. Have we learned enough about the way the mind and brain interpret the human environment so that we can understand the sources of beliefs? Do we know very much at all about the way non-rational beliefs get combined with various cultural attributes to produce particular anti-social attitudes? The "self-awareness" of humans in different environments has produced the enormous diversity of belief systems that have in the past been, and continue in the present and will continue in the future to be, the basic underlying source of human behavior. But we know all too little about the way such belief systems evolve, how they spread, and what are the consequences for human performance. The devastating implications of modern military technology make such understanding a necessary condition for human survival.

II

A central thesis of this study has been that the non-ergodic nature of our world poses problems for dealing successfully with the endless novelty that humans confront as they evolve ever more complex and interdependent human environments. There are two parts to this problem: how well the minds of the members of a society have evolved the adaptability to confront novel problems, and just how novel the problems are. It may be that some of the members of a society see the "true" nature of an issue but are not in a position to alter the institution. It is necessary that those who make the political decisions have such vision; yet it is not self-evident that the polity tends to "install" such people in the decision-making role.

167

The way the mind works is important: If evolutionary psychologists are correct that much of our behavior is genetically driven, just how flexible are humans in confronting novelty? The problems that humans face today and tomorrow bear little resemblance to those facing a hunter/gatherer individual. The degree of novelty obviously is a crucial determinant of our potential success in dealing with the problems. We tend to talk glibly about technological change, the internet, and genetic alteration as solutions to our problems without recognizing the new and novel problems that will result from the consequent alterations in the human environment. The interdependent world we are creating requires immense societal change and raises genuine problems about human adaptability.

III

The fall in information costs and open access of all societies to the performance of others has clearly accelerated institutional imitation and adaptability. But in spite of such accessibility the gap between developed and less developed countries continues to widen. Our understanding of the process of change set forth in the foregoing chapters makes clear that the process of catching up is a complicated one. We still do not know how to create polities that will put in place economic rules with the correct incentives. We still have a very incomplete understanding of the complex institutional and technologically interdependent structure of political economies which is necessary to improving their performance. The sobering story of our limited success in encouraging economic development in sub-Saharan Africa and in Latin America suggests that we have some distance to travel before we can have confidence in our institution building to improve performance. And the turmoil in the Muslim world (both within that world and between the Muslim world and its neighbors) has cast a deep shadow on the human prospect. The turmoil of Russia since the early 1990s is a sobering testimonial to the difficulties of constructing a new institutional framework that can work. A complicating factor is the process of change itself, which may make solutions derived from past experience unworkable in new and novel contexts. Economists hang on to a body of theory developed to deal with advanced economies of nineteenth-century vintage in which the problems were those of resource allocation. That theory, which economists persist in trying to adapt to fundamental problems of development, is simply inappropriate to deal with the issues of this study.

IV

All societies throughout history have eventually decayed and disappeared. Some like Rome have lasted for many centuries, others like the Soviet Union have lasted less than a century. Mancur Olson maintained that in the absence of periodic revolutions, interest groups tend to make societies rigid and to throttle the productivity improvement that lies behind growth. The brief story of the Soviet Union is a testimonial to the pitfalls inherent in an inflexible institutional framework. What I have termed adaptive efficiency is an ongoing condition in which the society continues to modify or create new institutions as problems evolve. A concomitant requirement is a polity and economy that provides for continuous trials in the face of ubiquitous uncertainty and eliminates institutional adaptations that fail to resolve new problems. Hayek made this condition a central part of his argument for human survival. It has certainly characterized United States's societal development over the past several centuries, even with all the blemishes that are a part of its history. An underlying source appears to have been the development of a set of informal institutional constraints that have been powerful restraints against rigid monopoly in all it guises. But their development was more good fortune than intent; and even if we knew their source, they evolved over a long period of time and do not appear to be replicable either deliberately or in a short time period. Moreover, there is no guarantee that the flexible, adaptively efficient institutional structure will persist in the ever more complex novel world that we are creating. The ubiquity of economic decline of civilizations in the past suggests that adaptive efficiency may have its limits.

Has the growth in the stock of knowledge made this dismal story obsolete? Some of the glowing predictions from think tanks wedded to science and technology as saviors would have one believe so; but it is a complex blend of the way consciousness evolves in the context of diverse human experiences that shapes human decision making. To understand the human condition it is essential to focus on the intentionality of the players. Economists have the correct insight that economics is a theory of choice. But to improve the human prospect we must understand the sources of human decision making. That is a necessary condition for human survival.

Bibliography

Abraham, Anita and Jean-Philippe Platteau. 2002. Participatory Development in the Presence of Endogenous Community Imperfections. Working Paper, University of Namur, Department of Economics.

Adelman, Irma and Cynthia Taft Morris. 1971. *Society, Politics, and Economic Development: A Quantitative Approach*. Baltimore: Johns Hopkins Press.

Alston, Lee and Andres Gallo. 2001. The Erosion of Legitimate Government: Argentina, 1930–1947. Working paper, University of Illinois.

Arrow, Kenneth J. 1951. Alternative Approaches to the Theory of Choice in Risk-Taking Situations. *Econometrica* 19(4), 404–37.

Arthur, W. Brian. 1992. On Learning and Adaptation in the Economy. Queen's Institute for Economic Research Discussion Paper 854 (May).

————. 1999. Complexity and the Economy. *Science* 284 (April 2), 107–9.

Arthur, W. Brian, Steven N. Durlauf, and David A. Lane. 1997. *The Economy as an Evolving Complex System II*. Reading, Mass.: Addison-Wesley.

Bairoch, Paul. 1988. *Cities and Economic Development*. Christopher Braider, trans. Chicago: University of Chicago Press.

Barkow, Jerome H., Leda Cosmides, and John Tooby. 1992. *The Adapted Mind: Evolutionary Psychology and the Generation of Culture*. New York: Oxford University Press.

Barro, Robert J. 1996. Democracy and Growth. *Journal of Economic Growth* 1(1), 1–27.

Barzel, Yoram. 1997. *Economic Analysis of Property Rights*, 2nd edition. Cambridge: Cambridge University Press.

Bates, Robert H., Rui J. P. de Figueiredo Jr., and Barry R. Weingast. 1998. The Politics of Interpretation: Rationality, Culture, and Transition. *Politics and Society* 26(4), 603–42.

Baumgartner, Peter and Payr Sabine, eds. 1996. *Speaking Minds: Interviews with Twenty Eminent Cognitive Scientists*. Princeton: Princeton University Press.

Bean, Richard. 1973. War and the Birth of the Nation State. *Journal of Economic History* 33(1), 203–21.

Bechtel, William and George Graham, eds. 1998. *A Companion to Cognitive Science*. Malden, Mass.: Blackwell.

Bechtel, William, Adele Abrahamsen, and George Graham. 1998. The Life of Cognitive Science. In William Bechtel and George Graham, eds. *A Companion to Cognitive Science*. Malden, Mass.: Blackwell.

Bendor, Jonathan and Piotr Swistak. 2001. The Evolution of Norms. *American Journal of Sociology* 106(6), 1493–546.

Benz, Ernst. 1966. *Evolution and Christian Hope: Man's Concept of the Future from the Early Fathers to Teilhard de Chardin.* Garden City: Doubleday.

Ben-Ner, Avner and Louis G. Putterman, eds. 1998. *Economics, Values, and Organization.* Cambridge: Cambridge University Press.

Boyd, Robert and Peter Richerson. 1985. *Culture and the Evolutionary Process.* Chicago: University of Chicago Press.

Boyer, Pascal. 2001. *Religion Explained: The Evolutionary Origins of Religious Thought.* New York: Basic Books.

Burnette, Joyce and Joel Mokyr. 1995. The Standard of Living through the Ages. In Julian L. Simon, ed. *The State of Humanity.* Cambridge, Mass.: Blackwell Publishers Inc.

Calvert, Randall. 1998. Explaining Social Order: Internalization, External Enforcement, or Equilibrium? In Karol Soltan et al., eds. *Institutions and Social Order.* Ann Arbor: University of Michigan Press.

Chomsky, Noam. 1975. *Reflections on Language.* New York: Pantheon Books.

Clark, Andy. 1997. *Being There: Putting Brain, Body, and World Together Again.* Cambridge, Mass.: MIT Press.

Clark, Andy and A. Karmiloff-Smith. 1993. The Cognizer's Innards: A Psychological and Philosophical Perspective on the Development of Thought. *Mind and Language* 8(3), 488–519.

Coleman, James. 1990. *Foundations of Social Theory.* Cambridge, Mass.: Harvard University Press.

Costa, Dora A. and Richard H. Steckel. 1995. Long-Term Trends in Health, Welfare, and Economic Growth in the United States. Historical Paper 76, NBER Working Paper Series on Historical Factors in Long Run Growth, November.

Cox, Gary W. and Matthew D McCubbins. 2001. Structure and Policy: The Institutional Determinants of Policy Outcomes. In Matthew D. McCubbins and Stephen Haggard, eds. *The Structure of Fiscal and Regulatory Policy.* Washington, D.C.: World Bank, Policy Research/Finance Division.

Damasio, Antonio R. 1999. *The Feeling of What Happens: Body and Emotion in the Making of Consciousness.* New York: Harcourt Brace.

David, Paul A. 1997. Path Dependence and the Quest for Historical Economics: One More Chorus of the Ballad of QWERTY. *Oxford University Discussion Papers in Economic and Social History* No. 20 (November).

Davidson, Paul. 1991. Is Probability Theory Relevant for Uncertainty? A Post-Keynesian Perspective. *Journal of Economic Perspectives* 5(1) (Winter), 129–43.

Davis, Lance E. and Douglass C. North. 1971. *Institutional Change and American Economic Growth*. Cambridge: Cambridge University Press.

Dawkins, Richard. 1998. *Unweaving the Rainbow: Science, Delusion, and the Appetite for Wonder*. Boston: Houghton-Mifflin.

Deevey, Edward S. 1971. The Human Population. In Paul R. Ehrlich, John P. Holdren, and Richard W. Holm, eds., *Man and the Ecosphere*. San Francisco: W. H. Freeman. Reprinted from *Scientific American* 203 (1960), 195–204.

De Figueiredo, Rui and Barry R. Weingast. 1999. Rationality of Fear: Political Opportunism and Ethnic Conflict. In Jack Snyder and Barbara Walter, eds. *Military Intervention in Civil Wars*. New York: Columbia University Press.

Demsetz, Harold. 1967. Toward a Theory of Property Rights. *American Economic Review* 57(2), 347–59.

Dennett, Daniel Clement. 1991. *Consciousness Explained*. Boston: Little Brown.

———. 1995. The Mystery of Consciousness. *New York Review of Books* 42(20), 83.

Denzau, Arthur T. and Douglass C. North. 1994. Shared Mental Models: Ideologies and Institutions. *Kyklos* 47(1), 3–31.

Denzau, Arthur and Paul Zak. 2001. Economics Is an Evolutionary Science. In Albert Somit and Stephen Peterson, eds. *Evolutionary Approaches in the Behavioral Sciences: Toward a Better Understanding of Human Nature*. New York: Elsevier.

De Roover, R. 1965. The Organization of Trade. In M. M. Postan, E. E. Rich, and Edward Miller, eds. *The Cambridge Economic History of Europe* 3. Cambridge: Cambridge University Press.

Diamond, Jared. 1997. *Guns, Germs, and Steel: The Fates of Human Societies*. New York: W. W. Norton and Co.

Donald, Merlin. 1991. *Origins of the Modern Mind: Three Stages in the Evolution of Culture and Cognition*. Cambridge, Mass.: Harvard University Press.

———. 1998. Hominid Enculturation and Cognitive Evolution. In C. Renfrew and C. Scarre, eds. *Cognition and Culture: The Archaeology of Symbolic Storage*. University of Cambridge: Monographs of the McDonald Institute for Archaeological Research, 7–17.

———. 2000. The Cognitive Foundations of Institutional Knowledge. Stanford University: Second KNEXUS Research Symposium, July 31–August 2.

———. 2001. *A Mind So Rare: The Evolution of Human Consciousness*. New York: W. W. Norton and Co.

Dopfer, Kurt, ed. Forthcoming. *Evolutionary Foundations of Economics*. Cambridge: Cambridge University Press.

Dosi, G., L. Marengo, and G. Fagiolo. Forthcoming. Learning in Evolutionary Environments. In K. Dopfer, ed. *Evolutionary Foundations of Economics.* Cambridge: Cambridge University Press.

Easterlin, Richard A. 1996 [1998 paperback]. *Growth Triumphant: The Twenty-first Century in Historical Perspective.* Ann Arbor: University of Michigan Press.

———. 1999. How Beneficent Is the Market? A Look at the Modern History of Mortality. *European Review of Economic History* 3(3), 257–94.

Edelman, Gerald M. 1992. *Bright Air, Brilliant Fire: On the Matter of the Mind.* New York: Basic Books.

Edelman, Gerald M. and Guilio Tononi. 2001. *Consciousness: How Matter Becomes Imagination.* London: Penguin Books.

Eggertsson, Thrainn. 1996. No Experiments, Monumental Disasters: Why It Took a Thousand Years to Develop a Specialized Fishing Industry in Iceland. *Journal of Economic Behavior and Organization* 30(1), 1–23.

———. 1998. Sources of Risk, Institutions for Survival, and a Game against Nature in Premodern Iceland. *Explorations in Economic History* 35(1), 1–30.

Elman, Jeffrey. 1998. Connectionism and Artificial Life. In William Bechtel and George Graham, eds. *A Companion to Cognitive Science*, 496. Malden, Mass.: Blackwell.

Elster, Jon. 1989. Social Norms and Economic Theory. *Journal of Economic Perspectives* 3(4), 99–117.

———. 1996. Rationality and the Emotions. *Economic Journal* 106(438), 1386–397.

———. 1998. Emotions and Economic Theory. *Journal of Economic Literature* 36(1), 47–74.

Elton, G. R. 1953. *The Tudor Revolution in England.* Cambridge: Cambridge University Press.

Ferdinand, P. 1992. Bukharin and the New Economic Policy. In A. Kemp-Welch, ed. *The Ideas of Nikolai Bukharin.* Oxford: The Clarendon Press.

Fogel, Robert W. 2003. *The Escape from Hunger and Premature Death 1700–2100: Europe, America, and the Third World.* Cambridge: Cambridge University Press.

Fogel, Robert W. and Dora L. Costa. 1997. A Theory of Technophysio Evolution, with Some Implications for Forecasting Population, Health Care, and Pension Costs. *Demography* 34(1), 49–66.

Greif, Avner. 1989. Reputation and Coalition in Medieval Trade: Evidence on the Maghribi Traders. *Journal of Economic History* 49(4), 857–82.

————. 1993. Contract Enforceability and Economic Institutions in Early Trade: The Maghribi Traders' Coalition. *American Economic Review* 83(3), 525–48.

————. 1994a. On the Political Foundations of the Late Medieval Commercial Revolution: Genoa During the Twelfth and Thirteenth Centuries. *Journal of Economic History* 54(2), 271–87.

————. 1994b. Cultural Beliefs and the Organization of Society: A Historical and Theoretical Reflection on Collectivist and Individualist Societies. *The Journal of Political Economy* 102(5), 912–50.

————. Forthcoming a. *Institutions: Theory and History*. Cambridge: Cambridge University Press.

————. Forthcoming b. Impersonal Exchange without Impartial Law: The Community Responsibility System. *Chicago Journal of International Law*.

Grossman, Gregory. 1998. Subverted Sovereignty: Historic Role of the Soviet Underground. In Stephen S. Cohen et al., eds. *The Tunnel at the End of the Light: Privatization, Business Networks, and Economic Transformation in Russia*. Berkeley: University of California International and Area Studies Digital Collection, Research Series #100, <http://repositories.cdlib.org/uciaspubs/research/100>.

Haber, Stephen, Armando Razo, and Noel Maurer. 2003. *The Politics of Property Rights: Political Instability, Credible Commitments, and Economic Growth in Mexico, 1876–1929*. Cambridge: Cambridge University Press.

Hahn, Frank H. 1987. Information, Dynamics, and Equilibrium. *Scottish Journal of Political Economy* 34(4), 321–34.

Hayami, Yujiro and Masahiko Aoki, eds. 1998. *The Institutional Foundations of East Asian Economic Development: Proceedings of the IEA Conference Held in Tokyo, Japan*. New York: St. Martin's Press; IEA Conference Volume, no. 127.

Hayek, F. A. 1952. *The Sensory Order: An Inquiry into the Foundations of Theoretical Psychology*. Chicago: University of Chicago Press.

————. 1960. *The Constitution of Liberty*. Chicago: University of Chicago Press.

————. 1979. *Law, Legislation, and Liberty*. London: Routledge and Kegan Paul.

Heiner, Ronald. 1983. The Origin of Predictable Behavior. *American Economic Review* 73(4), 560–95.

Henrich, Joseph, Robert Boyd, Samuel Bowles, Colin F. Camerer, Ernst Fehr, Herbert Gintis, and Richard McElreath. 2003. In Search of Homo economicus: Experiments in 15 Small-Scale Societies. *American Economic Review* 91(2), 73–79.

175

Hexter, J. H. 1992. Introduction. In J. H. Hexter, ed. *Parliament and Liberty from the Reign of Elizabeth to the English Civil War.* Stanford: Stanford University Press.

Hill, Kenneth. 1995. The Decline in Childhood Mortality. In Julian L. Simon, ed. *The State of Humanity.* Cambridge, Mass.: Blackwell Publishers Inc.

Hodgson, Geoffrey. 1993. *Economics and Evolution.* Ann Arbor: University of Michigan Press.

Hoffman, Elizabeth, Kevin McCabe, and Vernon Smith. 1998. Behavioral Foundations of Reciprocity: Experimental Economics and Evolutionary Psychology. *Economic Inquiry* 36(3), 335–52.

Hogarth, Robin M. and Melvin W. Reder, eds. 1987. *Rational Choice: The Contrast Between Economics and Psychology.* Chicago: University of Chicago Press.

Holland, John H. et al. 1986. *Induction: Processes of Inference, Learning, and Discovery.* Cambridge, Mass.: MIT Press.

Hughes, J.R.T. 1977. *The Governmental Habit.* New York: Basic Books.

Hutchins, Edwin. 1995. *Cognition in the Wild.* Cambridge, Mass.: MIT Press.

Hutchins, Edwin and Brian Hazelhurst. 1992. Learning in the Cultural Process. In C. G. Langston et al., eds. *Artificial Life II.* Redwood City, Calif.: Addison-Wesley.

Karmiloff-Smith, A. 1994. Precis of Beyond Modularity: A Developmental Perspective on Cognitive Science (with Peer Commentary). *Behavioral and Brain Sciences* 17(4), 683–745.

Keefer, Philip. 2002. Clientelism, Credibility, and Democracy. World Bank Working Paper (November).

Knight, Frank H. 1921. *Risk, Uncertainty, and Profit.* New York: Houghton Mifflin and Co.

Knight, Jack and Douglass C. North. 1997. Explaining Economic Change: The Interplay Between Cognition and Institutions. *Legal Theory* 3(September), 211–26.

Kremer, Michael. 1990. Population Growth and Technological Change: One Million B.C. to 1990. *Quarterly Journal of Economics* 108(3), 681–716.

Kuran, Timur. 1986. The Economic System in Contemporary Islamic Thought. *International Journal of Middle East Studies* 18(2), 135–64.

———. 1997. Islam and Underdevelopment: An Old Puzzle Revisited. *Journal of Institutional and Theoretical Economics* 153(1), 41–71.

———. 2003. The Islamic Commercial Crisis: Institutional Roots of Economic Underdevelopment in the Middle East. *Journal of Economic History* 63(2), 414–46.

Law, Marc and Sukkoo Kim. 2003. Specialization and Regulation: The Rise of "Professionals" and the Emergence of Occupational Licensing Regulation in America. Draft, Washington University in Saint Louis. Used by permission.

Lewin, Mosh. 1995. *Russia/USSR/Russia*. New York: The New Press.

Loasby, Brian J. 1999. *Knowledge, Institutions, and Evolution in Economics*. London: Routledge.

Lucas, Robert. 1981. Tobin and Monetarism: A Review Article. *Journal of Economic Literature* 19(2) (June), 558–67.

Lupia, Arthur, Samuel L. Popkin, and Mathew D. McCubbins, eds. 1999. *Elements of Reason: Cognition, Choice, and the Bounds of Rationality*. Cambridge: Cambridge University Press.

Macfarlane, Alan. 1978. *The Origins of English Individualism*. Oxford: Oxford University Press.

Maddison, Angus. 1995. *Monitoring the World Economy 1820–1992*. Organisation for Economic Co-operation and Development.

———— 2001. *The World Economy: A Millennial Perspective*. Organisation for Economic Co-operation and Development.

Maitland, Frederic W. 1963. *The Constitutional History of England: A Course of Lectures*. London: Cambridge University Press.

Manski, Charles F. 1996. Treatment under Ambiguity. Santa Fe Institute Working Paper No. 96–10–078.

Martens, Bertin. 1999. The Cognitive Mechanics of Economic Development: Economic Behavior as a Response to Uncertainty. Working Paper, Max Planck Institute.

————. 2004. *The Cognitive Mechanics of Economic Development and Institutional Change*. London: Routledge.

McCabe, Kevin. 2003. Reciprocity and Social Order: What Do Experiments Tell Us about the Failure of Economic Growth? Working Paper, George Mason University.

McCauley, Robert. 1998. Levels of Explanation and Cognitive Architecture. In William Bechtel and George Graham, eds. *A Companion to Cognitive Science*. Malden, Mass.: Blackwell.

McFaul, Michael. 1995. State Power, Institutional Change, and the Politics of Privatization in Russia. *World Politics* 47(2), January, 210–43.

————. 1999. Lessons from Russia's Protracted Transition from Communist Rule. *Political Science Quarterly* 114(1), 103–31.

————. 2001. *Russia's Unfinished Revolution*. Ithaca: Cornell University Press.

McGuire, Martin and Mancur Olson. 1996. The Economics of Autocracy and Majority Rule: The Invisible Hand and the Use of Force. *Journal of Economic Literature* 34(1), 72–96.

McKeown, Thomas. 1976. *The Modern Rise of Population.* New York: Academic Press.

Milgrom, Paul R., Douglass C. North, and Barry R. Weingast. 1990. The Role of Institutions in the Revival of Trade: The Law Merchant, Private Judges, and the Champagne Fairs. *Economics and Politics* 2(1), 1–23.

Miller, Gary. 1992. *Managerial Dilemmas.* Cambridge: Cambridge University Press.

Mitchell, Brian R. 1975. *European Historical Statistics 1750–1970.* London: Macmillan.

Mitchell, Brian R. 1983. *International Historical Statistics: The Americas and Australasia, 1750–1988.* London: Macmillan.

Mokyr, Joel. 1990. *The Lever of Riches.* New York: Oxford University Press.

———. 2000. Knowledge, Technology, and Economic Growth During the Industrial Revolution. In Bart Van Ark et al., eds. *Productivity, Technology and Economic Growth.* The Hague: Kluwer Academic Press.

———. 2002. *The Gifts of Athena: Historical Origins of the Knowledge Economy.* Princeton: Princeton University Press.

Mwabu, G., C. Ugaz, and G. White, eds. 2001. *Social Provision in Low Income Countries.* Oxford: Oxford University Press.

North, Douglass C. 1981. *Structure and Change in Economic History.* New York: W.W. Norton and Co.

———. 1990a. A Transaction Cost Theory of Politics. *Journal of Theoretical Politics* 2(4), 355–67.

———. 1990b. *Institutions, Institutional Change, and Economic Performance.* Cambridge: Cambridge University Press.

———. 1991. Institutions, Transactions Costs, and the Rise of Merchant Empires. In J. Tracy, ed. *The Political Economy of Merchant Empires.* Cambridge: Cambridge University Press.

———. 1994. Economic Performance through Time. *American Economic Review* 84(3), 359–68.

———. 1995a. Five Propositions about Institutional Change. In Jack Knight and Itai Sened, eds. *Explaining Social Institutions.* Ann Arbor: University of Michigan Press.

———. 1995b. The Paradox of the West. In R. W. Davis, ed. *The Origins of Modern Freedom in the West.* Stanford: Stanford University Press.

North, Douglass C. and Robert P. Thomas. 1973. *The Rise of the Western World.* Cambridge: Cambridge University Press.

North, Douglass C. and Barry R. Weingast. 1989. Constitutions and Commitment: The Evolution of Institutions Governing Public Choice in Seventeenth-Century England. *Journal of Economic History* 49(4), 803–32.

North, Douglass C., William Summerhill, and Barry R. Weingast. 2000. Order, Disorder, and Economic Change: Latin America *versus* North America. In Bruce Bueno de Mesquita and Hilton Root, eds. *Governing for Prosperity.* New Haven: Yale University Press.

Nove, Alec. 1969. *An Economic History of the U.S.S.R.* London: Allen Lane.

Olson, Mancur. 1982. *The Rise and Decline of Nations: Economic Growth, Stagflation, and Social Rigidities.* New Haven: Yale University Press.

Pinker, Steven. 1994. *The Language Instinct: How the Mind Creates Language.* New York: William Morrow and Company.

Pirenne, Henri. 1963. *Early Democracies in the Low Countries: Urban Society and Political Conflict in the Middle Ages and the Renaissance.* New York: Harper and Row.

Platteau, Jean-Philippe and Yujiro Hayami. 1998. Resource Endowments and Agricultural Development: Africa *versus* Asia. In Yujiro Hayami and Masahiko Aoki, eds. *The Institutional Foundations of East Asian Economic Development: Proceedings of the IEA Conference Held in Tokyo, Japan,* 357–410. New York: St. Martin's Press; IEA Conference Volume, no. 127.

Powell, Walter. 1996. Interorganizational Collaboration in the Biotechnology Industry. *Journal of Institutional and Theoretical Economics* 152(1), 197–215.

Power, Eileen. 1941 (1965). *The Wool Trade in English Medieval History.* New York: Oxford University Press.

Previte-Orton, Charles. 1960. *The Shorter Cambridge Medieval History,* vol. 1. Cambridge: Cambridge University Press.

Putnam, Robert D., Robert Leonardi, and Raffaella Nanetti. 1993. *Making Democracy Work: Civic Traditions in Modern Italy.* Princeton: Princeton University Press.

Rakove, Jack, Andrew R. Rutten, and Barry R. Weingast. 2001. Ideas, Interests, and Credible Commitments in the American Revolution. Working Paper, the Hoover Institution, Stanford University.

Roeder, P. G. 1993. *Red Sunset: The Failure of Soviet Politics.* Princeton: Princeton University Press.

Rosenberg, Nathan and L. E. Birdzell. 1986. *How the West Grew Rich.* New York: Basic Books.

Rosenberg, Charles. 1979. The Therapeutic Revolution: Medicine, Meaning, and Social Change in Nineteenth-Century America. In M. Vogel and C. Rosenberg, eds. *The Therapeutic Revolution.* Philadelphia: University of Pennsylvania Press.

Sacks, David. 1992. Parliament, Liberty, and the Commonwealth. In J. H. Hexter, ed. *Parliament and Liberty from the Reign of Elizabeth to the English Civil War.* Stanford: Stanford University Press.

Samuelson, Paul A. 1969. Classical and Neoclassical Theory. In Robert W. Clower, ed., *Monetary Theory*. London: Penguin.

Satz, Debra and John Ferejohn. 1994. Rational Choice and Social Theory. *Journal of Philosophy* 91(2), 71.

Searle, John R. 1997. *The Mystery of Consciousness*. New York: New York Review of Books.

Solnick, Steven. 1998. *Stealing the State*. Cambridge, Mass.: Harvard University Press.

Solow, Robert M. 1985. Economic History and Economics. *American Economic Review* 75(2) (May), 328–31.

Stiglitz, Joseph, T. Hellman, and K. Murdock. 1998. Financial Restraint and the Market-Enhancing View. In Yujiro Hayami and Masahiko Aoki, eds. *The Institutional Foundations of East Asian Economic Development: Proceedings of the IEA Conference Held in Tokyo, Japan*. New York: St. Martin's Press; IEA Conference Volume, no. 127.

Stubbs, William. 1896. *The Constitutional History of England*. Oxford: Oxford University Press.

Stufflebeam, Robert S. 1998. Representation and Computation. In William Bechtel and George Graham, eds. *A Companion to Cognitive Science*. Malden, Mass.: Blackwell.

Tawney, R. H. 1926. *Religion and the Rise of Capitalism*. New York: Harcourt Brace and Co.

Tooby, J. and L. Cosmides. 1992. The Psychological Foundations of Culture. In H. Barkow, L. Cosmides, and J. Tooby, eds. *The Adapted Mind*. Oxford: Oxford University Press.

Turner, Mark. 2001. *Cognitive Dimensions of Social Science*. Oxford: Oxford University Press.

U.S. Department of Commerce. 1976. *Historical Statistics of the United States, Colonial Times to 1970*. Washington D.C.: U.S. Govt. Printing Office.

U.S. Department of the Treasury. 2001. *Statistical Abstract of the United States*. Washington D.C.: U.S. Govt. Printing Office.

Vanberg, Viktor. 1994. *Cultural Evolution, Collective Learning, and Constitutional Design*. Dordrecht and Boston: Kluwer Academic.

Wallis, John Joseph and Douglass C. North. 1986. Measuring the Transaction Sector in the American Economy. In Stanley Engerman and Robert E. Gallman, eds. *Long-Term Factors in American Economic Growth*. Chicago: University of Chicago Press.

———. 1988. Should Transaction Costs Be Subtracted from Gross National Product? *Journal of Economic History* 48(3), 651–54.

Weber, Max. 1904 [1958]. *The Protestant Ethic and the Spirit of Capitalism.* New York: Scribner.

Weingast, Barry. 1998. Political Stability and the Civil War: Institutions, Commitment, and American Democracy. In Robert H. Bates, Avner Greif, Margaret Levi, Jean-Laurent Rosenthal, and Barry R. Weingast, *Analytical Narratives.* Princeton: Princeton University Press.

Weingast, Barry and William J. Marshall. 1988. The Industrial Organization of Congress; or, Why Legislatures, Like Firms, Are Not Organized as Markets. *Journal of Political Economy* 96(1), 132–63.

White, Lynn. 1978. *Medieval Religion and Technology.* Berkeley: University of California Press.

Williamson, Oliver E. and Scott E. Masten, eds. 1999. *The Economics of Transaction Costs.* London: Edward Elgar Publishing, Ltd.

Wilson, Edward O. 1998. *Consilience: The Unity of Knowledge.* New York: Knopf.

Witt, Ulrich. 1992. *Explaining Process and Change: Approaches to Evolutionary Theory.* Ann Arbor: University of Michigan Press.

Wohlgemuth, Michael. 2003. Democracy as an Evolutionary Method. In P. Pelican and G. Wegner, eds. *The Evolutionary Analysis of Economic Policy.* Northampton, Mass.: Edward Elgar.

Index

Abraham, Anita, 100
Act of Abjuration of Allegiance to Philip
    II, 142
Africa, 75; sub-Saharan, vii, 75, 119, 129,
    155, 160, 168
Antwerp, 134
Aoki, Masahiko, 58
Aragon, 144
Argentina, 125
Arrow, Kenneth, 13
Arthur, Brian, 70
Articles of Confederation, 110. *See also*
    U.S. Constitution
artificial intelligence, 30, 31
asymmetric information, 55
Augsburg, 129

Bangladesh, 99
Barro, Robert J., 57
Bean, Richard, 131
Bechtel, William, 32
beliefs, 2, 4, 8, 11, 23, 49, 50, 79, 83, 99,
    102, 116, 117, 146, 157, 166, 167; col-
    lectivist, 135–36; and consciousness,
    47, 103; and decisions, 117; of entre-
    preneurs, 126; formation of, 25; and
    institutions 49, 146; non-rational, 2,
    41, 56, 72, 102; and novel situations,
    69; and order, 104–5; and social con-
    text, 36; and uncertainty, 63
Benx, Ernst, 137
Black Death, 20
Bonaparte, Napoleon, 112
Boyer, Pascal, 41
Bremen, 129
Brezhnev, L., 150, 151

Buddhism, 58. *See also* religion
Burgundians, 142

Calvinism, 43, 135. *See also* religion
capital: human, 48–49, 94; physical, 48–
    49; social, 75
capital markets, 123, 125
Carolingian Empire, 129
Castile, 144
Catholicism, 38, 128, 135. *See also*
    religion
C-D gap, 14
Champagne Fair, 132
Charles V, 134
Charles VII, 131
checks and balances, 68. *See also*
    Madison, James
China, 88, 137, 159
Chomsky, Noam, 29, 31
Christianity, 58, 136, 137. *See also*
    religion
Clark, Andy, 24, 32
Coase, Ronald, 156, 165
coercion, 105
cognition, 25, 31, 33–34
cognitive science, 5
Coke, Sir Edwards, 143
Coleman, James, 75, 135
collectivism, 101
communism, 4
Community Responsibility System, 118
competence-difficulty gap. *See* C-D gap
computationalism, 31
Confucianism, 58
Congress. *See* U.S. Congress
connectionist models, 26, 30, 31, 72

183

consciousness, 4, 6, 38, 43, 44, 47,
103, 167; and conscience, 39–40;
core, 39; extended, 39, 40. *See also*
intentionality
Constantinople, 129
Constitution. *See* U.S. Constitution
contract enforcement, 159
cooperation, viii
Cortes, 142
Cosmides, L., 29
Costa, Dora, 96
Cox, Gary W., 52
culture, ix, 18, 30, 34, 46, 49, 50, 51, 69;
evolution of, 72; mimetic, 34; mythic,
34; oral, 34; theoretic, 34, 35, 74; variation in, 42

Damasio, Antonio, 37, 39, 45
Darwin, Charles, 38, 44, 65. *See also*
evolution
Davidson, Paul, 19
Davis, Lance, vii
De Figuerdo, 106
De Roover, R., 130
democracy, 56, 71
Demsetz, Harold, 57
Diamond, Jared, 88n.2
Donald, Merlin, 26n.5, 31, 35, 69
Dynegy, 122

Easterlin, Richard, 96, 99
economic revolution: first, 87;
second, 87
Edelman, Gerald M., 26, 40, 41
efficiency, 15
Eggertsson, Thrainn, 58
Elman, Jeffrey, 31
Elster, Jan, 58
Engels, Friedrich, 3, 148
England, 89, 107, 109, 137, 138, 143,
145; and British Empire, 108
Enron, 122

entrepreneurs. *See* organizations
environment, 28. *See also* uncertainty
epigenesis, 29
equilibrium, 23, 69
ergodic, 13, 19, 22, 163
Europe, vii, 112, 128, 129, 133–34;
western, vii, 78
evolution: biological, 6, 66; Darwinian,
viii, 6; economic, 66, 74; and psychology, 28, 29, 168
exchange: impersonal, 71, 84, 119;
market, 71; personal, 70, 84, 119

fanaticism, 45. *See also* beliefs; religion
Feldman, Julian, 27
Ferdinand and Isabella, 144
Ferejohn, John, 24
Fogel, Robert W., 95, 96
folk theorem, 29
France, 109, 131, 138, 140, 143
Franco, 144

Galileo, 44
game theory, 69
general equilibrium theory, vii. *See also*
neoclassical economic theory
Glorious Revolution, 118
Gorbachev, Mikhail, 4, 150, 153
Gould, Stephen J., 28, 71
government, 84, 123. *See also* state
Greif, Avner, 18, 69, 75, 118, 135
Grossman, Gregory, 151
guilds, 141

Hahn, Frank, 62
Hayami, Yujiro, 58, 59, 75
Hayek, Friedrich A., 5, 32, 33, 36, 42, 51,
56, 72, 73, 162
Hazelhurst, Brian, 50
Heiner, Ronald, 14
Henrich, Joseph, 47
Henry VIII, 143